The Naval Warfare of World War II: The History of the Ships, Tactics, and Battles that Shaped the Fighting in the Atlantic and Pacific

By Charles River Editors

The U.S.S. Yorktown fighting during the Battle of Midway, just as a torpedo hits the boat.

About Charles River Editors

Charles River Editors provides superior editing and original writing services in the digital publishing industry, with the expertise to create digital content for publishers across a vast range of subject matter. In addition to providing original digital content for third party publishers, we also republish civilization's greatest literary works, bringing them to new generations of readers via ebooks.

Sign up here to receive updates about free books as we publish them, and visit Our Kindle Author Page to browse today's free promotions and our most recently published Kindle titles.

Introduction

The USS *Arizona* exploding during the attack on Pearl Harbor

The Naval Warfare of World War II

Naval combat underwent a significant metamorphosis during World War II. Nazi Germany and Imperial Japan launched some of the most powerful battleships ever to sail the world's oceans, yet the conflict witnessed the emergence and triumph of the aircraft carrier as the 20th century's true monarch of the seas. Submarine warfare expanded and developed, while aircraft technology and doctrine experienced several revolutionary changes due to the unforgiving demands of the new combat environment.

Popular accounts of World War II frequently focus on the dominance of German panzers over the more lightly armored, lightly armed tanks of the Soviets, British, and Americans, or the superb fighting skills of the Waffen SS and ordinary Wehrmacht soldiers. Germany's land forces enjoyed an undoubted advantage over their enemies thanks to excellent vehicle technology, while German soldiers slaughtered vast numbers of Soviet conscripts and proved formidable opponents even to their better-trained English and American counterparts.

However, the Axis failed to secure either the seas or the skies, and their defeat in these theaters ultimately led to their doom. Many highly advanced aircraft designs languished on the drawing boards of Junkers and Messerschmitt engineers, left undeveloped due to high command disinterest or simple lack of resources. The most advanced fighters developed by Nazi Germany and Imperial Japan were equaled or outmatched by such aircraft as the U.S. F6F Hellcat (which achieved kill ratios of between 13 to 1 and 19 to 1 against Japanese "Zero" fighters) or P-51 Mustang.

America, with its vast productive resources and immense manufacturing capacity, single-handedly supplied the materiel that saved Britain and the Soviet Union from defeat. It did so by controlling the sea lanes and eventually ending much of the threat of U-boat attack, supplying England and Russia with staggering quantities of food, weapons, raw materials, trucks, tanks, aircraft, prefabricated buildings, boots, ammunition, medicines, and even entire locomotives and sets of railway rolling stock. Over 50% of the Soviet Union's entire wartime supply base, from food and clothing to weapons and vehicles, came directly from the United States.

In time, the American and British navies progressively destroyed their Axis counterparts, ensuring clear sea lanes, high strategic mobility for seaborne invasions, and large-scale air support that eventually battered the Axis armies into submission. Just as the Luftwaffe paralyzed Poland's defenders in 1939 with air superiority, so the Allies' mastery of naval and aerial warfare turned the tables to paralyze the Nazis and Japanese: "The fate of Germany and Japan was sealed [...] by the many-layered application of Anglo-American air and sea power. The totality of this pressure [...] eventually choked off Axis mobility. [...] Air and sea power could operate throughout the productive process, not only to affect the battlefield, but to determine how much and what kinds of military equipment were produced and deployed." (O'Brien, 2015, 480).

Indeed, the "ultimate weapon" of World War II proved to be not a powerful tank or a specific type of aircraft, but a gigantic piece of military hardware combining the newly augmented power of both air and naval operations, the aircraft carrier. Every diverse element of the military machine had a crucial role to play, but the aircraft carrier stood head and shoulders above any other single system as the key to victory in the mid 1940s.

The Naval Warfare of World War II: The History of the Ships, Tactics, and Battles that Shaped the Fighting in the Atlantic and Pacific looks at the course of the fighting in the Atlantic and Pacific during the war, and the changes both sides made in an effort to establish supremacy. Along with pictures of important people, places, and events, you will learn about the naval warfare of World War II like never before.

The Naval Warfare of World War II: The History of the Ships, Tactics, and Battles that Shaped the Fighting in the Atlantic and Pacific

About Charles River Editors

Introduction

    Chapter 1: Fighting in the Atlantic

    Chapter 2: Naval Forces and Doctrines in the Pacific Before Pearl Harbor

    Chapter 3: The Battle of the Java Sea

    Chapter 4: Opposing Naval Forces

    Chapter 5: The Doolittle Raid and Coral Sea

    Chapter 6: Midway

    Chapter 7: Japan's Last Gasp

    Chapter 8: The End of the War

    Chapter 9: The Legacy of Naval Warfare during World War II

    Online Resources

    Bibliography

Chapter 1: Fighting in the Atlantic

A picture of British officers on a destroyer that's part of a convoy

The Battle of the Atlantic represented an arms race on multiple levels, including both offensive weapons systems and defensive countermeasures. While the Allies honed their convoy technology and improved its use, the Germans added new features to their U-boats, enabling them to move faster, hit harder, and attempt to escape after an attack in a more effective manner. The back-and-forth exchange witnessed the Germans discovering a fresh weakness, exploiting it, and then, after a brief period of notable success, losing ground to new countermeasures. In this race, the Allies eventually outpaced the Axis, leading to the effective defeat of the U-boats and their reduction to a mere annoyance later in the war.

The stakes of this naval struggle remained very high throughout the war. America's control of the sea lanes provided Britain with food and weaponry, while the Lend-Lease program supplied the Soviets with materiel without which their defeat would have been nearly assured. Alongside tens of thousands of trucks, locomotives, tanks, cars, motorcycles, artillery pieces, 15 million pairs of boots, 14 billion pounds of food (much of it high-calorie processed meat), and countless rounds of ammunition, the Americans also supplied the USSR with a wide range of raw materials, brought in by sea.

Without U.S. control of the sea lanes, the Soviets would have foundered, as the American supply of one vital metal – aluminum – to their quasi-hostile allies demonstrates: "The Soviet Union, however, was desperately short of aluminum. When Harry Hopkins paid his first visit to Josef Stalin in July 1941 to ask the Soviet dictator what the country needed to keep fighting in light of the German invasion, the number one priority he was given was immediate aluminum shipments so that the Soviet Union could build more aircraft. From then until the end of the war, the United States poured aluminum into the Soviet Union. By 1943 it was providing the Soviets more of the metal then was actually allocated to the entire United States Navy." (O'Brien, 2015, 64).

In abandoning the creation of aircraft carriers, the Nazis unwittingly gave up any chance of truly controlling the Atlantic. The U-boats struck like ambush predators, and certain classes of land-based aircraft joined the fray also, but the German lack of aircraft carriers crippled their ability to carry out modern fleet actions and achieve decisive victory at sea.

The Allied commanders already knew from shipping experiences in World War I that large convoys of ships offered a poor target for U-boats. Escorts protected such aggregations of vessels more effectively, concentrating their defensive force and providing mutual support. Therefore, in World War II, convoys provided the rule, not the exception, from the beginning. Though the Germans gained some signal triumphs nevertheless, and nearly halted shipping at a few points, the convoy system married to technological and tactical advances ultimately prevailed.

Even such an apparently simple factor as improving cargo ship engines offered the Allies major dividends. The American and British planners grasped very early that even an extra 1 to 2 knots in speed made a tremendous difference in vessel survivability. Accordingly, the Americans built their Liberty Ships to travel at a then-rapid 11 knots. Over 38 million tons of Liberty Ships launched from American shipyards, amounting to 2,710 ships and overwhelming the U-boats' best efforts by speed and numbers.

As part of the overall strategic plan, Allied command utilized rational statistical analysis, providing invaluable insights into the mathematics behind one of the many factors blending into Anglo-American success in the Battle of the Atlantic: "The Americans ended up calculating the safety difference of convoys in 1943. [...] One American calculation was that increasing the speed of a convoy from 7 knots to 9 knots gave the ships involved an extra one-third as much protection from German submarine attack.. [...] between October 1942 and May 1943, the faster convoys (those averaging around 9 knots) suffered a 50 percent smaller casualty rate than slower convoys (those averaging around 7 knots), even when they were attacked at approximately the same rate." (O'Brien, 2015, 255-256).

A picture of a merchant ship after being torpedoed by a German submarine

The Germans also utilized surface ships, known as commerce raiders, to strike at the convoys with both cannons and torpedo fire. While it might seem incredible that surface vessels operated openly near the mighty Royal Navy and its constant air patrols, the Nazis managed this trick for some time through clever use of camouflage.

The Germans quickly added and removed false, light wooden structures such as merchant ship funnels or cargo storage bins to rapidly change the appearance of their surface raiders. The British aircraft crews and sailors displayed an almost touching naiveté in the manner in which they accepted some of the Germans' visual hoaxes at face value: "The crews were also trained to wear civilian clothes on deck, and usually there were special 'characters' designed to make the vessel appear more harmless to a casual observer, such as a 'woman' pushing a baby carriage on deck. German disguises fooled British patrols again and again. On May 18, 1941, the *Atlantis* – disguised as a Dutch freighter – passed within 8,000 yards of the British battleship HMS *Nelson* without arousing suspicion." (Forczyk, 2010, 42).

The Germans also set afloat several huge battleships, including the *Bismarck* and the *Graf Spee*. These colossal ships, intended to devastate whole convoys unsupported or with only a handful of other raiders accompanying them, inflicted some damage but ultimately fell victim to their own overwhelming presence. Viewing them as an outsized threat, the British poured all available resources into hunting these battleships down, and their size rendered the ships slow and difficult to hide, sealing their fate once the British successfully pinpointed them with scouting aircraft.

The Bismarck famously encountered the British battleships HMS *Hood* and *Prince of Wales* shortly after dawn on May 24th, 1941, but at first the Germans believed the contact to be a much smaller ship. However, the aggressive *Hood* quickly disabused them of the notion: "The fore guns of the Hood woke with a tremendous thunder, the wind swept a huge cloud of black cordite smoke over the bridge and four shells, each weighing more than 800 kilograms, began the 23,000 metre-long journey towards the intended target. All German doubts disappeared as the Hood's guns fired, almost immediately followed by the main guns of the Prince of Wales. The huge muzzle flashes and the long firing range were signs clear enough." (Zettering, 2012, 156).

The *Bismarck*

HMS *Hood*

Following a brief, lethal duel, a probable magazine explosion blew the *Hood* apart, causing it to sink with tremendous loss of life. The Bismarck's crew, however, did not long survive to savor their triumph; brought to battle by four British vessels just three days later on May 27th, 1941, the battleship sustained 400 direct hits by shells out of 2,800 fired at it by the English. Seeing his ship set ablaze and unable to escape, the captain ordered the *Bismarck* scuttled, but the British rescued only 111 men before retreating, frightened off by a false report of U-boats approaching. Some 2,200 luckless German sailors drowned or died of exposure in the cold North Sea waters, proving the diminished value of battleships.

The *Graf Spee* suffered a similar fate during the Battle of the River Plate in South America. However, Nazi Germany's chief weapon prowled not above the waves, but beneath them. The U-boats, used to devastating effect in World War I, returned in an updated form for World War II. In time, over 200 of these craft scoured the Atlantic for targets, striking without warning before slipping away to elude depth charges and other forms of retaliation.

From almost the moment when Britain declared war on Germany following Hitler's 1939 invasion of Poland through 1943, U-boats plied the Atlantic waves, attempting to disrupt Britain's American lifeline. American and Canadian vessels escorted the convoys partway across the ocean before handing over guard duty to British ships. At first, America's lack of war status with the Axis powers ensured this arrangement. Later, the grim but diplomatic U.S. Admiral Ernest J. King continued the practice both to make use of valuable British assets and to respect the patriotic feelings of the English.

American support of Great Britain, amounting to a de facto declaration of war against Nazi Germany and the Axis even before Pearl Harbor, enabled the English to remain in the war. Without the weapons, supplies, and material sent across the Atlantic to England, Hitler might perhaps have compelled Winston Churchill's government to accept peace and leave the continent to its Nazi masters. Winston Churchill summed this situation up when he declared "the only thing that really frightened me during the war was the U-boat peril" (Williamson, 2007, 4).

Nazi Germany's chief answer to the endless convoys streaming across the Atlantic to support its British foes lay in its submarine fleet of U-boats. The Germans, curiously, never developed a fleet of aircraft carriers. The Kriegsmarine began construction of two, the Graf Zeppelin and the Peter Strasser, but completed neither. Two others never achieved any reality beyond blueprints, while the conversion of a cruiser into the carrier *Weser* began but failed to reach completion.

In the struggle against the packs of U-boats, the Anglo-American forces used any and all means at their disposal. Included in their arsenal, some 133 blimps cruised the skies above the Atlantic, shepherding convoys of supply ships, transports, and Liberty Ships and performing valuable scouting missions while conserving fuel.

The Americans' use of zeppelin escorts, the K-ships, to protect convoys and drop depth charges on attacking U-boats, remains little-known today. Nevertheless, the long, gleaming, neoprene-coated balloons of the K-ships slid through the Atlantic skies above many convoys between early 1942 and the end of the European war in mid-1945. During this time the zeppelins escorted some 70,000 surface ships and carried out numerous scouting expeditions during more than 37,000 individual sorties.

K-ships, built by Goodyear Aircraft Company and powered by a pair of Pratt & Whitney engines attached to propellers, measured around 250 feet long. Cruising at 58 miles per hour (though frequently matching the much slower speed of a surface convoy), these bloated, silvery airships could reach 78 miles per hour in an emergency. Each carried a .50 caliber machine gun for defense, alongside a rack of 350-lb depth charges.

Though the K-ships lacked sufficient room in their gondolas to take survivors of successful U-boat attacks on board, they still offered useful aid to such men. They reported the position of occupied lifeboats or individual sailors to craft capable of retrieving these survivors, and carried supplies of food and water they lowered to men in lifeboats, increasing their chances of survival markedly.

Enthusiastic K-ship crews frequently reported dropping their depth charges on enemy submarines, often confidently noting they had identified these as German or Italian based on clues known only to themselves. Regardless of their relative effectiveness, the zeppelins provided a unique morale boost to Allied seamen: "The men of the merchant marine [...] knew that, like their own vessels, surface escorts were vulnerable to underwater attack. The blimp was not. Airplanes, of course, were not vulnerable either, but they came and went in a hurry [...] The blimp stayed with the convoy, flying low and throttling back to keep a slow pace. [...] Airship crews and merchant ship crews waved to each other, the airship looking all the while majestic and overwhelmingly powerful and reassuring." (Vaeth, 1992, 68-69).

In fact, no confirmed record of a U.S. zeppelin sinking a U-boat exists, though the gleefully vigorous dropping of depth charges probably inflicted some unrecorded minor damage over the course of 4 years of war. Additional specialized types, such as the G-ship, the L-ship, and the M-ship joined the roster as the war progressed.

In addition to whatever damage they inflicted, the airships spotted many German submarines, directing other, faster-moving assets to the area and frequently prompting a retreat or causing the occasional kill. These American Goodyear zeppelins affected German morale as well; later U-boat survivor testimonies suggest that the packs of submarines hesitated to approach a convoy shadowed by the gleaming, oblong shape of a blimp, whose ongoing presence bespoke sleepless vigilance.

Other than occasional instances when circumstances allowed them to produce unusual devastation among the convoys, the U-boats of the Kriegsmarine never mustered sufficient force to fully stop the Atlantic convoys. The advent of the Liberty Ships made this event even less likely, given their numbers and relatively high speed. However, Germany's submarines exacted a toll of shipping, materiel, and lives that the Allies found increasingly unacceptable as the tally mounted.

The turning point arrived in 1943. In March of that year, the U-boats' success rose to a crescendo with the sinking of 108 ships (amounting to over 675,000 tons), while the Germans only suffered minimal losses. Yet, in the months immediately following, the situation reversed entirely and the Allies swept the ocean clear of U-boats.

The key to success, besides increased experience and coordination between ships, aircraft, and other assets, lay in a small, powerful technological device. Two British scientists, Harry Boot and Dr. John Randall, invented a microwave radar device dubbed the "resonant cavity magnetron." This device, so small the British and Americans easily fitted it to a wide range of aerial and surface vehicles, generated short-wave radar capable of resolving incredible detail dozens of miles away. Even better from the Allied point of view, the U-boats' radar detectors only picked up long-wave radar, meaning the Nazi submarines could not tell when the microwave radar device "painted" them.

Introduced to field operations on a large scale in April 1943, the resonant cavity magnetron immediately and decisively shifted the tide of conflict in the Atlantic in favor of the Allies. Combined with a massive shipbuilding program on the part of the United States, including the production of 30-plane compact aircraft carriers for escort duty and destroyer escorts with speeds up to 24 knots (cutting-edge for their day), the new technology dealt a body blow to the U-boat efforts from which the Kriegsmarine never recovered. The Axis lost 15 U-boats in April while dealing only 277,000 tons of damage to the convoys, less than half of the previous month's total at a greater cost in submarines. In May, 41 U-boats sank, a crippling blow to a force consisting of just 230 vessels in total, with monthly production peaking at 23 U-boats in the North German shipyards.

The Germans realized the Allies outmatched them when they captured one of the new devices. Damaged beyond use, the Germans nevertheless managed to build a replica for testing: "When a German model at last was completed, it was tested at the top of a radio tower with results that flabbergasted the testers. In spite of low visibility, objects 20 miles distant showed up on the radar screen in extraordinary detail. Among those present at the test was a delegation from the German Navy; […] they 'took one look at the radar set and knew why there had been such dreadful U-boat losses during the past months.'" (Pitt, 1977, 186).

As U-boats continued to perish at a spiraling rate, Admiral Karl Donitz ordered the submarines to abandon the Atlantic struggle on May 24th, 1943. Though he lied to Hitler and stated the offensive would resume in a few weeks, the Admiral knew the Kriegsmarine had lost to the Anglo-American forces. The U-boats only sank 92 ships over the entire year between Donitz's retreat and the D-Day landings in June 1944.

Donitz

In fact, plans for the D-Day landings would begin almost immediately after the Allied commanders realized the U-boats turned tail. Carriers such as the USS *Bogue* continued combing the Atlantic waters for intruders, but the days of the commerce raiders had ended. American Admiral Ernest J. King and British Admiral Sir Max Horton collaborated on developing a grand naval strategy during 1942, into 1943, and onward, which led to victory at sea and eventually on the European continent also.

Once the U-boat menace subsided and the Germans lost the capacity to build a powerful surface fleet, the European war's conclusion became foreordained. Neither the British nor the Soviets would succumb with the tremendous support offered by the industrial complexes and vast interior farmlands of the United States. As the Allies cemented control of the skies, the Germans increasingly suffered the same fate they inflicted on the Poles in the first days of the war. The Allies bombed factories, destroyed new tanks and vehicles in crippling numbers before the Germans managed to bring them into action, and cut off almost all large-scale transport of vital supplies and fuel.

Eventually, the Anglo-American air forces denied the Germans even local tactical movement, annihilating panzer or mechanized units from the air if they sought to move during the day. Even the famous Ardennes Offensive occurred in foul weather, crashing to a halt immediately when skies cleared and the flights of Spitfires, Mustangs, and Hellcats once again scoured the landscape like steel eagles watching keenly for prey.

Chapter 2: Naval Forces and Doctrines in the Pacific Before Pearl Harbor

"Before we're through with them, the Japanese language will be spoken only in Hell." - Vice Admiral Halsey

Oil and atrocities lay at the heart of Japan's conflict with the United States. Alliance with Nazi Germany and Fascist Italy cast the Japanese in a semi-hostile role towards the Americans in any case, but the incredible barbarity of the Imperial Japanese Army in China incensed and disgusted the United States, in addition to threatening some Chinese trade.

At the Rape of Nanking, the Japanese killed over 250,000 people. Tens of thousands of women suffered rape, many killed by having foreign objects such as bayonets or sharpened bamboo stakes stabbed fatally into their genitals by the Japanese soldiers upon completion of the act, or literally raped to death – violated by so many men in succession that they bled to death from internal ruptures. Even Nazi German observers expressed horror at the mass torture and massacre, seeking vainly to save the lives of at least some Chinese slated for shooting, beheading, or live burial. The Japanese also sank an American gunboat attempting to evacuate civilians from Nanking, killing most of its crew, though the Imperial government claimed an accidental sinking and paid reparations, defusing a potential early start to the war.

Disgusted by Japanese war crimes and anticipating future hostilities with the belligerent Empire, the Americans cut off their fuel trade with the Japanese. The United States had no desire to provide the very logistical support enabling Japanese butchery in China and a possible eventual threat to America and its ally, Australia. The Japanese obtained 20% of their fuel from Japan itself or the East Indies: "The remainder, 80 percent, came from the United States. [...] In July 1940, the United States prohibited export of high-grade aviation fuel [...] to Japan [...] It was not so much that the Americans were tired of seeing their exports to Japan being turned against the Chinese, although they were, but that they strongly suspected that their exports to Japan were about to be turned back on themselves." (Cox, 2014, 23).

While the Americans refused to resume oil exports until the Japanese withdrew from their conquests, the Japanese remained equally determined. Essentially, the Japanese wished to become a superpower along the lines of America, Britain, Germany, or the Soviet Union, and retreat would relegate it to a lower status than its leaders accepted. The Japanese concepts of "face" and "shame" also prevented them from backing down from their high water mark.

The loss of American oil supplies pushed the Japanese into a desperate step. The Imperial high command slated Java, Borneo, and Sumatra for conquest, adding the rich oil fields to their list of assets and rendering American fuel imports superfluous. The American presence in the Philippines, however, placed a potentially hostile force directly in between the Javan and Sumatran oil fields and Japan itself.

The Japanese decided that seizure of the Philippines from the Americans would eliminate this possible threat. A tissue of fantasies about the American reaction to this attack encouraged the Imperial government to complete this fatal step. The Japanese believed that destroying the ships at Pearl Harbor would prevent American naval operations in the Pacific for at least several years, during which time the United States would decide the Philippines and the sneak attack constituted insufficient cause for a full-scale war.

In a sanguine mood, the Empire's planners anticipated an eventual return to peace and normalization of relations with America, including resumption of trade and U.S. oil exports to Japan, while Japan retained full control of China, the oil fields in Java, Sumatra, and Borneo, the Philippines, and other conquests. They had some reason to be confident, because by 1941, the Japanese navy was one of the most capable in the world and so formidable that it was equaled only by the American and British navies. At that point, however, both of those nations were heavily committed in the Atlantic and Mediterranean respectively.

Japan's navy was a well balanced and modern force, building on a recent but highly successful naval tradition. Japan had only emerged from relative isolation during the 19th century, but as an island nation it had a cultural affinity for the sea and a strategic appreciation of its importance. In fact, Japan had unashamedly turned to the world's premier naval power for advice on modern naval thinking. In 1912, the Russo-Japanese war, which had stagnated on the ground at Port Arthur, was decisively resolved in Japan's favor by means of the massive sea battle of Tsushima. The Japanese had used modern British-built ships with British advisors onboard to smash the antiquated Tsarist fleet. With that, Japan had arrived as a naval power.

Although Japan served as a useful British ally during World War I, Japan spent its time between the wars evolving its own forward-thinking naval doctrine, and it also had the industrial capacity and designers to produce highly sophisticated modern warships. Thus, by 1941 Japan's battleships and aircraft carriers were among the best in the world, and, representing thinking which had diverged radically from their British mentors, the Japanese had pioneered the carrier task force. It was that kind of fleet which would land the devastating blow at Pearl Harbor - six aircraft carriers in all, as many gathered for one operation as Britain had deployed across the entire globe.

Though Japan had invested extensively in naval airpower, the overall fleet was still well-balanced with state of the art heavy and light cruisers, as well as battleships. Like American battleships, Japan's battleships were based off the "bigger is better" philosophy so heavily influenced by Alfred Mahan, but overall her ships were light and fast, lacking the endurance and armor of those in the more traditional American fleet yet still packing a heavy punch. In fact, the Imperial Japanese Navy was highly trained for high-tempo night surface actions, with an emphasis on large salvoes of long range torpedoes. Indeed, despite the success of its operation at Pearl Harbor, the Japanese High Command truly longed for a Tsushima-style decisive surface action with the Americans which they believed might determine the outcome of the war. It has often been pointed out that the American carriers' absence from Pearl Harbor ultimately spelled Japan's doom, but the attack on Pearl Harbor was heavily focused on hitting the battleships that Japan perceived as the key index of naval power. This was all straight out of Mahan's textbook, but the Japanese would learn in 1942 at Midway that Mahan's strategies were befitting of an earlier era. Notwithstanding this mixed doctrine, Japan had a well-balanced, well-trained, experienced and modern fleet with which to confront America and the Allies. What she did not have was the resource base necessary to conduct extended operations.

Japan's *Yamato* was the biggest battleship in the world in 1941.

Like the Japanese, the U.S. Navy had also invested in aircraft carrier technology and doctrine. When World War II broke out, America had the world's second largest navy, but like Britain (and unlike Japan) it was deployed globally, including a big presence in the Atlantic. Like Japan (and unlike Britain), the U.S. Navy was beginning to explore the use of carrier fleet operations that ran contrary to Britain's mixed carrier/battleship approach. Japan and the U.S. had therefore drawn the same conclusion about the aircraft carrier; they could be a striking arm in themselves rather than a mere supplement to the main battle-fleet.

How did the Japanese and Americans reach a conclusion so at odds with the British, who had ruled the seas for centuries? The answer could largely be attributed to an understanding that the Pacific theater was devoid of bases from which to launch planes. Thus, any air cover over the fleet would therefore need to be carrier-based, and more importantly an all-carrier force would have the freedom to operate without worrying about land-based enemy aircraft. The Pacific offered the canvas on which the aircraft carrier battle group could really prove its worth. Unfortunately for the U.S., it would be Japan that first proved that fact.

Despite reaching a similar conclusion regarding carrier based operations, inter-war debate within the U.S. had in one sense been on the opposite trajectory of that in Japan. The American experience was shaped by the need to cut costs and maintain a modest peace-time navy just sufficient to deter conflict. If conflict came, it was initially thought that the likely opponent would be Britain or some other enemy in the Atlantic. In Japan of course, a militaristic and expansionist junta was pushing for the biggest fleet it could get. The arms-racing which had contributed so much to the momentum for war earlier in the century haunted the great democracies. This resulted in the American-sponsored Washington naval treaties of the 1920's and 30's, which sought to constrain naval armament across the globe.

The result was a fleet which remained battleship-based but was beginning to expand its carrier component, albeit trailing Japan's bold initiatives. And a lot of the ships were rather old compared to Japan's state of the art new builds. However, before 1941 America was aware of the security risk posed by their earlier failure to invest. The Vinson-Walsh Act of 1940 was pivotal, approving the building of 25 capital ships, 18 of them carriers, and the measure was approved by 316 votes to 0 in the House of Representatives. If Japan was to secure a decisive advantage over the U.S. Navy and exercise political leverage in the Pacific, she needed to do so before these new ships came online. This was another critical component in the analysis that pushed Japan towards attacking Pearl Harbor.

While the U.S. went about expanding its navy, the military went about putting plans in place to confront Japan in the Pacific. Plan Orange specifically addressed a possible war with Japan and had been evolving since before World War I. It envisaged a strategic withdrawal to San Diego, while the U.S. Navy could be built up and strengthened, followed by a progressive counter-offensive. This was conservative but also realistic. It assumed short-term Japanese superiority and accepted that the Hawaiian Islands and Philippines would have to hang on - and possibly face invasion - in the absence of the main battle fleet. These were not concessions that were easy to make politically, and General Douglas MacArthur would vocally make the case for a stronger, more proper defense of the Philippines.

While that step was not forthcoming, Roosevelt did have the main Pacific fleet sent to Pearl Harbor, where it was meant as a deterrent to let Japan know the U.S. meant business. At the same time, however, stationing the Pacific fleet at Pearl Harbor meant the U.S. was potentially leaving the Philippines exposed, and American military planners were constantly in fear of a Japanese attack there in late 1941.

What is clear is that by stationing the Pacific fleet at Pearl Harbor, the U.S. did not have the ability to seriously contest a Japanese incursion into the Southern Resource Area in 1941. In other words, the U.S. could not actively prevent Japanese attacks against British Malaya or the Dutch East Indies. The decision to station the navy in Hawaii might very well have also signaled that Roosevelt had no intention of seriously contesting such an attack either. Thus, just what action Roosevelt would have taken in response to a Japanese attack on British Malaya or the Dutch East Indies without a corresponding attack on Pearl Harbor or the Philippines can rightly be considered one of history's great "what if's".

Though the attack on Pearl Harbor in December 1941 came as a great surprise and is still considered a daring strategy over 70 years later, such an attack had been contemplated by the Japanese High Command as early as 1927, and in 1928 Captain Isoroku Yamamoto had proposed such an attack in a lecture he gave at the Navy Torpedo School. During the 1930s, as Japan built up its navy and expanded across Asia, the concept of a strike against the U.S. Pacific Fleet gained momentum, and the Japanese had war-gamed such an attack on a number of occasions. What they had concluded was that they could expect heavy casualties, particularly if the Americans detected the Japanese fleet as it moved into position, and they were also worried about their ability to destroy battleships in harbor due to the difficulties of running torpedoes in shallow water. In overcoming that seeming disadvantage they were inadvertently aided by Britain following her successful strike against the Italian navy at Taranto, which relied exclusively on airpower.

Captain Yamamoto

In February 1941, when the Japanese High Command took the momentous decision to plan in earnest for a surprise attack on the American base at Pearl Harbor, it was with a view to delivering this psychological and political shock. In other words, Japan intended to deliver a message to the American people, not the American military. There was nothing new to this strategy so far as Japan was concerned; Japan's military doctrine emphasized the "will to fight" at all levels, and it had previously begun a war against Russia with a surprise assault at Port Arthur.

However, once the decision was made, Japanese planning was somewhat rigid and contradictory, both at the strategic and tactical levels. At the strategic level, it is possible to trace a number of competing ideas that lay behind Yamamoto's proposed assault at Pearl Harbor. The dominant one was his own notion that such an attack might predicate a quick return to the negotiating table. Indeed, he even went so far as to famously say, "If we fail at Pearl Harbor, we'd better give up the war". In this he seemed to recognize that if the conflict was dragged out, America would prevail on the strength of its resources. Another important concept for the Japanese was to shield their southern advance to Malaya and the East Indies, which they believed required wounding the U.S. Pacific fleet sufficiently so as to prevent its intervention. As noted earlier, however, current U.S. planning was conservative, and such a move was unlikely anyway.

A third was that the Japanese hoped to defeat the U.S. Navy in a decisive, Mahan-style "Tsushima" engagement, but crippling the American fleet at Pearl Harbor was likely to reduce the chances of the Americans making a large scale sortie that would bring on such an engagement. They were more likely to recover their losses, wait until they had secured superiority over Japan, and only advance westwards at that stage, just the kind of defensive strategy American planners had already concocted and what ultimately transpired.

Tactically, Japanese plans were even more confused. They identified four different missions for their aircraft on the day and chose to treat these almost as entirely separate events. On top of that, these problems were compounded, even as the carrier fleet was en route, by different opinions and instructions within the attacking units. Naval aviators felt that American carriers should be the priority target, but they were more aware of the potential power of this new weapons system than traditionalists. Conversely, Yamamoto was anxious to hit the battleships in accordance with his views on America's "will to fight"; and powerful elements within the Imperial Navy urged an emphasis on hitting American aircraft to help secure the safe withdrawal of the Japanese fleet. These tensions were never fully or clearly resolved, and to this day there is still debate over the precise instructions given to the pilots on the morning of December 7.

Within this framework of competing ideas, the four separate missions within the attack plan were a) torpedo bomber attacks on the battleships; b) medium level bomber attacks on the same battleships; c) dive bomber attacks on the carriers; and d) attacks on U.S. military aircraft and airbases. At the end of September 1941, with six weeks to go before the planned attack, Japanese naval air units were dispersed to a series of land airbases across the country for an intensive training period. Aircraft types and missions were kept separate in accordance with the specialized roles envisaged as outlined above.

The aircraft carriers of the U.S. Pacific Fleet were a specific concern of Mitsuo Fuchida, who led the Japanese air wing. It seems likely that it was his input during planning that led to the allotment of a large proportion of the dive-bombing force to this role. There were three carriers attached to the fleet - *Lexington*, *Saratoga* and *Enterprise*, but as fate would have it the carriers wouldn't be at Pearl Harbor that day. *Saratoga* was currently at San Diego, while *Lexington* and *Enterprise* were at sea. Therefore, plans to attack them became redundant, though the Japanese were not to learn that until the day prior to the attack. Had they been moored at Pearl Harbor, the high accuracy of the Aichi D3A "Val" dive bombers, coupled with the unarmored flight decks of the American flattops, would likely have resulted in substantial damage if not outright losses.

Fuchida

The Japanese opened the Pacific Theater's naval warfare in dramatic fashion with their stunning yet transitory victory at Pearl Harbor. Yamamoto's plan to attack Pearl Harbor, carried out with dedicated professionalism despite his immense personal doubts, delighted the Japanese. However, they opted not to seek the absent American carriers *Enterprise* and *Lexington*, failed to destroy the harbor's service facilities, and left the American submarines untouched in their pens. The sinking of 5 battleships and 13 other vessels, together with the deaths of 2,403 Americans, shocked the United States but served little military function other than to hasten reprisals.

In the wake of Pearl Harbor, Allied and IJN naval forces met in a notable naval encounter at the Battle of the Java Sea. Douglas MacArthur, in command of all forces in the Philippines, worked at cross purposes to Admiral Thomas C. Hart, the local USN chief. His superiors even rebuked him for his destructive intransigence. Admiral Hart sought in good faith to work with MacArthur to prepare the Philippines for invasion, but MacArthur rejected every overture with open belittlement and insults. Instead, he stated, he would meet the Japanese with 200,000 Filipino troops he would somehow raise, train, and equip in the few weeks left to him, and break Imperial Japan in a decisive land battle. Admiral Hart responded by "privately call[ing] MacArthur 'erratic' and 'no longer altogether sane ... he may not have been for a long time'" (Cox, 2014, 41) – perhaps a mild judgment from a man openly insulted in the grossest terms by MacArthur for months preceding the events of December 1941.

Though English defense centered around Singapore rather than the Philippines, Air Chief Marshal Robert Brooke-Popham showed a talent for muddled thinking quite the equal of Douglas MacArthur's: "The air marshal would try to obtain modern aircraft, but would, in response to a question from a reporter [...], explain his lack of such aircraft in terms infamous for their arrogance and stupidity: 'We can get on all right with Buffalos out here, but they haven't got the speed for England; let England have the 'super' Spitfires and the 'hyper' Hurricanes. Buffalos are quite good enough for Malaya.'" (Cox, 2014, 46).

With such individuals in positions of high command, the competent members of the Allied leadership in this vital theater found themselves hard put to it to organize an effective defense against the anticipated Japanese attack. Winston Churchill put the finishing touch to the coming fleet encounter between elements of the IJN and a combined Allied force of the United Kingdom, the United States, the Netherlands, and Australia when he sent the battleship HMS *Prince of Wales* to the region.

The English Prime Minister, indulging in what a British naval commander described as plans "conceived in Mr. Churchill's strategical cloud cuckoo land," estimated that the *Prince of Wales* and a few other Allied cruisers and destroyers could frighten the IJN away from Singapore and the Philippines.

On December 6th, 1941, the day prior to Pearl Harbor, British scouting aircraft spotted two huge Japanese naval convoys advancing across the South China Sea in the direction of Singapore and the Philippines. On December 8th, Japanese aircraft devastated American airplanes left on the ground at Clark Field near Manila, leaving the Japanese with air superiority over the Philippines.

MacArthur spent the larger part of the day ignoring his command as he sat in his pajamas in a "cataleptic" state, mired in a mental or emotional collapse – or perhaps simply a paralysis of fear – and unable to issue orders during the critical hours when the Japanese wiped out his air assets. After fleeing to Australia, MacArthur launched a series of profoundly toxic attacks and character assassinations, seeking to shift all blame for the catastrophe onto the subordinates who had attempted to salvage the situation despite the lack of unifying orders from their paralyzed commander.

Though British and Sikh pilots managed to defend Khota Baru on the night of December 8th, the Japanese invasion went ahead, and Singapore, the Philippines, and other Allied posts eventually fell. In the meantime, the *Prince of Wales* and another British battleship, plus three destroyers, played a deadly cat and mouse game with the Japanese swarming throughout the East Indies' seaways.

While Churchill and his cabinet held leisurely discussions over fine wine and good food during the course of several days as to what should be done with the *Prince* and its sister ships, like characters in a P.G. Wodehouse *Jeeves* novel, the actual vessels navigated the eastern waters in an attempt to interrupt Japanese seaborne landings while evading destruction themselves.

The small group of powerful British surface ships, dubbed Force Z, turned towards Kuantan on December 10th, hearing rumors of a Japanese attack they hoped to interrupt. On the same morning, Japanese Admiral Matsunaga sent out a powerful force of 37 bombers and 61 torpedo carriers to comb the seas near Kuantan for Force Z. Japanese submarines and scout aircraft reported the British ships in the vicinity over the past several days, and the IJN Admiral decided to bring them to battle.

No Japanese troopships were, in fact, attacking Kuantan. Nevertheless, the British commander, Admiral Phillips, dawdled in the area for hours while checking on a lone fishing trawler. His crews felt increasing fear as the *Prince of Wales* and the other ships remained largely immobile in potential close proximity to hostile carriers. As a man named Woods described the situation: "As expected, HMS *Express* returned shortly afterwards, reporting 'All is quiet as a wet Sunday afternoon.' I began to feel uneasy about all this. We were now sitting ducks if an air attack was launched. And it was a relief to leave the area though on our way out we investigated a suspicious looking tug that'd been spotted on reaching Kuantan as it was towing, what looked like troop carrying barges." (Cox, 2014, 92).

The delay to check the puny barge for a hidden Japanese invasion army proved Force Z's undoing. Hoashi Masame, an ensign in the Genzan Air Group, observed the British flotilla and radioed its position to his superiors. Though Force Z detected the radio transmission, the British airfield at Singapore – still able to send up supporting aircraft – did not, remaining idle throughout the coming encounter.

Force Z soon spotted Japanese bombers inbound. Admiral Phillips, ham-handed to the last, ordered the flotilla to turn hard to starboard, turning most of his anti-aircraft guns out of line with the attacking aircraft. Then, panicking, Phillips ordered a hard turn to port, as he realized his initial error. However, by this time, the British crews had adjusted many of their anti-aircraft guns to the starboard angle of firing. The port turn masked many of the guns afresh and threw off the aim of the remainder.

The Japanese bombers largely missed, however, inflicting only slight damage. Phillips ordered the ships to act independently if the Japanese returned, a wise order somewhat mitigating his earlier blunder. However, the next wave of Japanese aircraft carried a more devastating type of ordnance. 17 torpedo bombers under a Commander Nakanishi swooped in towards the British ships. Though Admiral Phillips initially refused to believe the Japanese fielded torpedo bombers against his command, the IJN pilots swiftly disabused him as they dove close to the heaving ocean surface and unleashed their fatal payload: "These Japanese bombers were indeed carrying torpedoes, in this case the deadly Type 91 aerial torpedo, weighing about 800kg (1,763lb), with a warhead of approximately 150kg (330lb). They were set to run at a blazing 42 knots, which they could do for a full 2,000m (2,190yd). As it would prove throughout the war, the Type 91, like most of the excellent Japanese torpedoes, was a devastating weapon unmatched in Allied arsenals." (Cox, 2014, 94).

Under the noon sun, the British found themselves unable to stop the Japanese torpedo bombers, which moved at 180 mph. Many British anti-aircraft guns jammed, and the defenders shot down only one Mitsubishi aircraft. A desperate turn caused most of the torpedoes to miss, but one struck just beside the *Prince of Wales*' gigantic propeller. The propeller and its shaft tore loose, twirling and shredding the ship's innards to admit vast quantities of seawater.

A radio signal finally reached Singapore and British aircraft prepared to take off at 12:20 p.m. However, a fresh Japanese attack occurred at approximately the same moment. The new wave carried Model 2 Type 91 torpedoes, with a bigger warhead at 450 lbs. The *Prince,* its engines dead and guns jammed, took four more hits, which punched gaping holes in its hull well below the waterline.

The other major ship, the *Repulse,* fought back more effectively, sending a number of Japanese aircraft into the sea, yet suffered four torpedo strikes within 5 minutes. With its hull blown apart, the *Repulse* rolled over on its side, then sank gently under the water, allowing a large number of its crew to take to life rafts, though many also died.

A picture of *Prince of Wales* and *Repulse* under attack during the fighting on December 10

A minute or two later, the *Prince of Wales* suffered a bombing attack that finally inflicted fatal damage. The HMS *Express,* a destroyer, came alongside to help rescue its crew, though Admiral Phillips, maintaining his character to the end, radioed to Singapore to send tugboats and destroyers, and signaled the *Express* to ask why it approached his ship so closely, to which F. J. Cartwright, commander of the *Express,* replied laconically, "it looks as though you require assistance."

Partway through the evacuation, the *Prince of Wales* capsized violently, taking Admiral Phillips to his death along with many of his men. Aircraft from Singapore arrived just in time to see the ship's underbelly glistening in the sun and then witnessed the ocean swallow the mighty ship whole. The destroyers managed to rescue hundreds more survivors from the water, but Phillips simply vanished. The next day, a Japanese pilot, Lieutenant Iki, flew over and dropped two bouquets on the site, one to honor the Japanese shot down and one to salute the courage of the British.

The destruction of these two powerful ships proved again how air power dominated ordinary surface vessels. The Americans realized the lesson fully, and the British almost as completely, but the Japanese – whose aircraft proved the point so forcefully – never completely abandoned the concept of the battleship, perhaps due to the conservatism underpinning their violently authoritarian culture: "The fate of Force Z was something new in the annals of naval war, and it settled old and bitter arguments. Though it was a Japanese victory and a painful Allied defeat, it was also a conceptual triumph within naval circles [...] for the cause of aviation, [...] Fleet doctrine would be hastily rewritten: battleships would now be relegated to a support role within task forces built around aircraft carriers. Their antiaircraft weaponry would be doubled, tripled, and finally quadrupled." (Toll, 2011, 76).

Chapter 3: The Battle of the Java Sea

The Battle of the Java Sea, following in early 1942, witnessed a continued use of surface ships unsupported by aircraft carriers. The Japanese prompted the battle by sending two huge invasion forces in a seaborne pincer movement to take Java. A mixed Allied force under the overall command of Dutch rear admiral Karel Doorman, a man with a prominent nose and slicked-back hair – who, as a pilot in his younger days, carried out 33 emergency landings successfully – moved to intercept the Eastern Invasion Force. The force hoped to sink the transport ships, drowning the Japanese soldiers aboard.

The Allies mustered 2 heavy cruisers, 3 light cruisers, and 9 destroyers, comprising Dutch, British, Australian, and American elements. Of the two heavy cruisers, one flew the British flag – the HMS *Exeter* – and the other the American – USS *Houston*. Doorman commanded from a light cruiser, the HNLMS *De Ruyter.* This detachment bore the name "Combined Striking Force."

The invasion force, embarked on 10 transports, used 14 destroyers, 2 light cruisers, and 2 heavy cruisers for defense. Rear Admiral Takeo Takagi, a man destined to command during the Battle of the Coral Sea and die at Saipan under uncertain circumstances, led the flotilla. Each Japanese heavy cruiser bristled with ten 8-inch guns compared to the six found on each Allied heavy cruiser, while Japanese torpedoes outranged Allied torpedoes by miles and moved at notably higher speeds.

A final advantage of the Japanese torpedoes lay in their oxygen propellant, which left no wake on the surface. Allied torpedoes, at this stage of the war, used steam propellant, producing a long streak of bubbles showing their precise path.

On the 26th, Doorman's Combined Striking Force sailed haphazardly across the Java Sea, attempting to find the Japanese in poor weather conditions. Several Japanese aircraft appeared, seeking to bomb the destroyer *Jupiter* and ignoring the larger ships nearby, a bizarre decision on the pilots' part. The small, nimble destroyer eluded the falling bombs, and anti-aircraft fire eventually caused the desultory Japanese attack to peter out.

On the 27th, another Japanese bombing raid targeted the *Jupiter*, making the choice of targets even more inexplicable. Once more, the bombs entirely missed the vessel. Close to 1 PM, Doorman decided to break off the search, citing the complete exhaustion of his crews. The Combined Striking Force retired into a gap between two Allied minefields. However, an hour later, reports started arriving from reconnaissance craft indicating a large Japanese surface force nearby.

Recklessly, Doorman turned the *De Ruyter* into one of the minefields in order to bring the vessel about as quickly as possible. The other ships followed after slight hesitation, attempting to sail in the wakes of the vessels ahead of them to avoid lurking mines. By some miracle, none of the vessels struck a mine, and by 3 PM, Doorman's force steamed rapidly towards the reported coordinates of the Japanese.

The fleet's mood combined vengeful aggression and eagerness with a paradoxical expectation of defeat. Nevertheless, the Allies started their venture against the Japanese with some of the pomp and ritual more associated with the 18th century than the 20th: "The crews of the American ships were stunned to see the British unfurl the flag that they traditionally only flew in battle, the giant White Ensign [...] It was universally described as awe-inspiring, a point of pride for everyone. Several of the ships also played music. Standing out in particular so that everyone could hear it was the song blaring from the loudspeakers of the *Exeter*: 'A Hunting We Will Go.' (Cox, 2014, 264).

The Japanese convoy, using ill-disciplined commercial vessels as transports, straggled over 20 miles of ocean. The Japanese Admiral, Takagi, allowed the majority of the escort to trail the convoy by many miles, leaving four destroyers and a light cruiser to defend the transports. When aerial scouts detected the approach of the concentrated Combined Striking Force at 3:10 PM, the convoy guards evinced both alarm and fury at being left to fend off a locally superior force while their leader, nicknamed "King Kong," cruised languidly far to the rear with most of the Eastern Invasion Force's firepower.

Faster, better armed, and considerably better armored than the obsolete craft under Doorman, the Japanese prepared to meet the Dutch-led attackers head on. Two more Japanese ships caught up before battle joined, further evening the odds. Though neither side possessed true air support, the Japanese seaplanes served as spotters for the guns on the surface ships, radioing back data enabling the gunners to adjust their aim effectively.

Doorman placed his ships into column for the attack, but did so in an unusual way, placing the cruisers with their long-range guns in front and the short-range destroyers at the rear. Before he could close with the transports, a Japanese light cruiser and swarm of destroyers appeared from the northeast, and two heavy cruisers – including the flagship of Admiral "King Kong" Takagi – also arrived.

Doorman's Combined Striking Force found itself in a problematic position. Slower than the Japanese fighting craft, the Allied ships risked Takagi's vessels "crossing their T" – sailing broadside across the front of their column and striking each ship in turn with their full firepower while the Allied ships could only reply with a few forward gun turrets. Doorman opted to move off at a slant, which prevented the Japanese from "crossing his T" but also kept the vessels far apart, where the Japanese guns, with superior range, held an advantage. Both sides fired constantly with their guns, but achieved no hits initially.

Between 4:30 and 4:50 p.m., the Japanese launched a huge salvo of torpedoes which failed to connect with even a single Allied hull. The continuing series of near misses continued as three Allied A-24 aircraft swooped over the scene, dropping bombs on one of the Japanese transports but failing to score a hit or even cause it to alter course. The Battle of the Java Sea illustrates clearly the limitations of World War II's "open sights" naval targeting systems, in which sheer volume of firepower provided the only solution to poor accuracy until a Japanese innovation towards the conflict's end.

A picture of the *Exeter* under attack

A picture of Japanese aircraft attempting to bomb a Dutch cruiser during the battle

The Combined Striking Force attempted to respond with torpedoes, but discovered the Japanese torpedoes far outranged their own. Confusion reigned as Doorman issued orders in Dutch, which, translated and transmitted on various kinds of equipment, arrived at the British, American, and Australian ships at different times and in different sequence. The Allied command started to dissolve into a chaotic jumble.

The whole Striking Force responded to Doorman's eventual command to turn about, however, and disaster finally struck. Another shoal of Japanese torpedoes arrived just as the Allied vessels turned broadside, presenting enormous targets to the incoming ordnance. While many of the torpedoes missed nevertheless, or collided with one another and exploded harmlessly, a direct hit blew the Dutch destroyer *Kortenaer* in half. The ship's halves sank in a matter of seconds, many men still visible clinging desperately to the wreckage, and one unknown sailor waving his comrades forward to attack the Japanese and avenge the destruction of his vessel.

Trapped by faster ships on the open Java Sea, unable to respond to IJN vessels able to hit them from 9 miles distant with torpedoes, the desperate Allied vessels charged in an effort to bring their foes within effective range. The maneuver cost the Allies the destroyer *Elelktra* but achieved little more.

As darkness fell, the Combined Striking Force initially retreated rapidly towards the coast of Java in the southeast, temporarily breaking contact with the IJN. At this point, Doorman detached the four American destroyers and sent them to Surabaya to refuel and rearm, since the prolonged fight exhausted their fuel and torpedo stocks alike. The destroyers took no further part in the Battle of the Java Sea, but also owed their accidental salvation to this circumstance.

Under cover of night, Doorman led the rest of his command back toward the Japanese. The Dutch admiral hoped to bypass the superior IJN naval assets in the dark and get in among the transports, sending them to the bottom along with tens of thousands of Japanese soldiers. This triumph failed to materialize. One British destroyer, the HMS *Jupiter*, struck a friendly mine and, catastrophically shattered, sank. The Dutch minelayer *Gouden Leeuw* (Golden Lion) laid the mines but failed to notify Doorman's command of the new minefield. 84 men on board died; the Japanese capture 97, and 83 more either reached the Javanese shore in life-rafts or were rescued by the American submarine S38.

As Doorman's small fleet attempted slipping past the Japanese destroyers and cruisers, prowling seaplanes illuminated them with flares. The IJN sank most of the remaining ships with gunfire and torpedoes, including the flagship, killing Doorman himself in the process: "Thirteen minutes later, the *De Ruyter* exploded with a mighty thunderclap of sound and broke in two. The fires quickly reached her magazine and set off a secondary explosion that briefly lit up the entire seascape for miles around. The two separated sections of her hull slipped quickly beneath the waves, taking 367 men, including Admiral Doorman, to the bottom. […] The sailors on the decks of the Japanese cruisers leaped and danced and shouted, "Banzai!" (Toll, 2011, 244-245).

Only two cruisers, the *Houston* and *Perth,* survived the catastrophe, and attempted to escape the area. However, on February 28th, 1942 at Bantam Bay near the western limits of Java, the American and Australian vessels came upon the anchored transports of the Western Attack Convoy.

Unable to resist so choice a target, the captains agreed to attack the transports. Swarmed by defending IJN ships, the *Houston* and *Perth* went to the bottom, yielding nearly 700 prisoners to the Japanese. Ironically, most damage to the transports came from overshooting Japanese torpedoes, including one which sank a transport outright and nearly drowned the Imperial 16th Army chief, General Hitoshi Imamura.

The Battle of the Java Sea cleared this strategic body of water of all Allied surface vessels, transforming it for the time being into a Japanese lake. The battle also represented the last major World War II fleet action in which direct fire weapons, such as 8-inch guns and ship-launched torpedoes, decided the outcome. Every other battle featured carrier versus carrier actions, with the flattops usually far beyond visual contact with one another.

Chapter 4: Opposing Naval Forces

Whereas other belligerents focused almost exclusively on land weaponry – tanks, artillery, trucks, self-propelled guns, and the like – the Japanese directed their industrial muscle towards developing a powerful fleet centered on aircraft carriers. Like the Kriegsmarine, the IJN (Imperial Japanese Navy) built several battleships with staggering line-of-sight firepower, which ultimately proved a useless waste of resources and which perished with their crews while inflicting no losses on the enemy. However, the IJN also realized the aircraft carrier's usefulness and gradually switched their strategy and tactics to favor this decisive weapons system: "Merchant and naval vessel construction received half of all the finished steel Japan produced between 1943 and 1945. Between 1942 and 1944, the Japanese finished the construction of one battleship [...], 13 aircraft carriers, 5 cruisers, 55 destroyers and 99 submarines. As a point of comparison, the United Kingdom in these years completed 2 battleships [...], 6 aircraft carriers, 15 cruisers, 141 destroyers and 111 submarines. […] these production profiles were quite similar." (O'Brien, 2015, 63).

Though the Soviets made 32 tanks for every Japanese tank produced, and the armored fighting vehicles they manufactured exhibited marked superiority in both protection and armament, the Japanese grasped the same strategic vision as the Americans and British. They aimed to control both strategic and tactical movement via naval and aerial dominance. The Japanese also perceived the Americans as their main potential enemy in their plan to dominate Asia and the Pacific, and they had aimed to put the Americans at a critical disadvantage via their preemptive strike on Pearl Harbor.

At the same time, Pearl Harbor demonstrated the power of aircraft carriers to launch devastating attacks on enemy assets located far outside the range of any friendly land-based airstrip, and the Americans developed their carrier doctrine rapidly in response to the newly-launched war: "The primary task of the carrier was now to destroy opposing carriers as soon as possible, thus preventing their own destruction and setting the stage for intensive attack on the enemy battle fleet. To maximize the carrier's striking power, standard US Navy doctrine called for the launch of an entire air group at one time. In order that an entire 'deck load' strike be launched quickly, it was necessary to have the entire strike spotted on the flight deck." (Stille, 2007, 9).

The American carriers proved a thorn in the IJN's side almost immediately following Pearl Harbor. These vessels demonstrated their strategic striking potential and ability to project power deep into enemy territory with a series of bombing raids on Japan in early 1942. These raids inflicted scant damage, yet cheered the American public and ordinary service personnel, while shaming the IJN command and eventually goading them into risky fleet actions such as Midway.

Both America and Japan made extensive use of carriers in the Pacific, fielding numbers of these mighty vessels unrivaled by other world powers. Only the British came close to equal reliance on the aircraft carrier. American industry, operating from a larger industrial base than Japan's and immune to interference from enemy bombers, churned out Essex-class carriers such as the USS *Ticonderoga*, of which the United States built 24, and the Midway class.

Japanese carriers showed considerable sophistication for their time, but also reflected a different doctrine from the Americans'. Their flattops utilized armored flight decks, which gave the ships a high center of gravity. To prevent easy capsizing and other stability problems, Japanese carriers featured smaller flight decks than American carriers of the same tonnage. The Japanese loaded less aircraft per unit of deck area, also, again to avoid excessive top-heaviness.

The armored deck resisted many types of hit, and Japanese technicians repaired it rapidly in the event of non-fatal damage. However, Japanese carriers also suffered from weak anti-aircraft armament and poorly designed fire extinguishing- procedures. The Japanese retained the 25mm cannon as a primary anti-aircraft weapon long after the Americans switched over to the quad 40mm Bofors gun.

25mm shells often glanced harmlessly off the thick armor on later U.S. aircraft designs such as the F6F Hellcat or the P-51 Mustang. 40mm shells, by contrast, tore the unarmored Zero fighters to pieces in midair whenever the American guns achieved a hit. USN anti-aircraft gunner training included marksmanship, emphasizing aiming and achieving hits with accurate fire. IJN training focused on "barrage firing," elevating "spray and pray" fire discipline to an expected norm for the AA guns defending Japanese flattops.

IJN carriers relied on hard pipe foam distribution systems for firefighting to a much greater extent than their United States counterparts. The Americans used manned hoses extensively, spraying either fire-smothering foam or water. Many fires on damaged IJN vessels burned out of control, causing internal explosions wrenching the ship apart from the inside. After Midway, no American carriers succumbed to fire, not even that started by kamikaze pilots with fuel-laden Zeros. While flight deck or bridge island damage might be extensive, the fire crews brought most blazes under control rapidly and, even in extreme cases like the USS *Ticonderoga*, managed to save the ship.

United States aircraft carrier design eschewed armored steel flight decks in favor of teak flight decks. Though this appears as a lower-tech solution at first glance, American carrier doctrine provided a solidly logical reason for this arrangement. Teak decks shattered easily when struck, and, though the crew repaired minor damage with planks stockpiled on board, a major kamikaze or bomb strike often necessitated a retreat to the United States for refitting. The Americans located the armored deck one level lower, with a much thicker, heavier hangar deck than IJN or Royal Navy flattops.

A lightweight teak flight deck and a heavyweight hangar deck gave American aircraft carriers a much lower center of gravity. This permitted a larger flight deck, overhanging the sides of the hull and giving space for a much larger complement of aircraft. In some cases, U.S. carriers supported twice the number of aircraft found on British or Japanese carriers of exactly the same weight.

American aircraft carriers, thanks to their large aircraft complements on light teak decks, punched far above their weight relative to their IJN opponents. These high concentrations of aircraft suited U.S. flattops ideally to a highly aggressive strategy, able to provide massive local air superiority and support devastating long-range strikes depending on the situation. Given that the Americans repeatedly overwhelmed their Japanese opponents from Midway onward, the design justified itself with practical success.

Teak decks provided one other fringe benefit. Teak, unlike plain steel and practically every other type of wood, retains good traction characteristics even when thoroughly wet. This characteristic gave American aircraft taking off or landing in stormy conditions a small but useful edge in managing the maneuver safely. Fire crews also found it easier to keep their footing on teak decks even when awash in foam and water.

Though Japanese carriers operated according to a far-sighted strategic doctrine and included many sophisticated features, the U.S. Navy managed to hit upon a winning formula that ultimately saw the IJN driven from the Pacific waters and the Japanese reduced to relying on suicide attacks in a futile, costly bid to keep the "Amerika-jin" at bay.

Moreover, even though the Japanese realized and seized upon the potential of the aircraft carrier as a powerful, high-tech naval weapon permitting bolder strategies than ever before seen in naval warfare, IJN thinking remained wedded to the idea of battleships offering the ultimate seaborne weapon. With the exception of one commander who voiced the perspicacious opinion that the "super battleships" merited only scrapping to use their material for more aircraft, the Japanese clung to the notion that a huge ship with big guns still ruled the waves with fanatical, irrational tenacity.

The result of this misplaced faith was the construction of the Yamato-class super battleships. Awe-inspiring vessels measuring 862 feet in length – practically the size of an Essex-class aircraft carrier – with a beam of 127 feet and a displacement of 73,000 tons fully loaded, these floating fortresses could sail 7,200 nautical miles without refueling. Armed with nine 18-inch guns, a dozen 6-inch guns and a dozen 5-inch guns, these oceangoing giants boasted armor plate up to 26 inches thick.

The Japanese actually completed two super battleships, the *Yamato* and the *Musashi*, while deciding to convert a third, the *Shinano*, into an aircraft carrier. Eventually upgunned even more, these vessels formed part of a dramatic IJN vision of a way to destroy the American fleet never practically tested, though used as the basis for a gigantic, costly construction program and the fate of over 5,000 men crewing these titans: "Once the torpedoes had done their work, the battleships would assume a parallel course some 38,000 yards distant from the enemy battle line and begin to fire with the aid of spotter aircraft. The Japanese assessed that the combination of massive torpedo attack and battleship gunnery would cause extensive damage to the American fleet. [...] while these complex plans looked viable in the halls of the Naval Staff College [...] they were never tested in their entirety in fleet exercises." (Stille, 2008, 7).

The *Yamato* and *Musashi*

Actual Japanese battleship performance, even among lighter, more maneuverable versions than the *Yamato* and *Musashi*, lagged far behind the rosy visions of IJN planners. Japanese battleships sank a few American vessels, including a handful of light aircraft carriers, but the usual result of an encounter saw few Japanese hits and a blistering response from American aircraft and, in some cases, radar-controlled guns.

Musashi and *Yamato* survived a remarkably long time during the war thanks to their gigantic slabs of armor plating, which provided protection far beyond any other vessel in the world at the time except perhaps for the similar, and equally ill-fated, Bismarck. However, their contributions to actual naval operations remained trivial at best, inflicting little damage compared to other weapons systems. Ironically, their most effective role emerged as that of target, drawing enemy firepower away from other fleet assets while possessing the resilience to shrug off much of the damage, but even in this function, their value remained dubious. The forces they accompanied lost, though the super battleships initially escaped this doomed encounters through near immunity to most aerial weapons.

In 1943, the *Musashi*, named for a province in central Japan, furnished perhaps its most notable service in functioning as a Brobdingnagian floating catafalque returning Admiral Yamamoto's cremated remains to Japan in suitable style.

A hint of *Musashi's* fate came in April 1944 when the American submarine *Tunny* blew a 19-foot hole in the ship's prow with a single torpedo, necessitating a return to port and extensive repairs. By the end of the war, the *Musashi* would demonstrate that an "unsinkable" ship does not exist.

Chapter 5: The Doolittle Raid and Coral Sea

The Americans would turn the war in the Pacific around in the middle of 1942, but in the wake of Pearl Harbor and the Japanese invasion of the Philippines, the country was in desperate need of a morale boost, and it would come in the form of the Doolittle Raid. In part to show that the Japanese were not invincible, and in part to reassure the American public that the nation would not lose the war, the Doolittle Raid included both Army and Navy units that launched 16 land-based medium bombers from an aircraft carrier, a feat that was the first of its kind but also one involving a great deal of risk. Getting the bombers and carriers in place to execute the mission involved much strategic planning and cooperation within the American military, and had it failed, it could have dealt a serious blow to the Americans' Pacific presence due to the nation's limited resources in that theater.

As if getting in position wasn't challenging enough, the raid was never designed to include a round trip back to the carrier. Given the size of the bombers, the planes were unable to land back on the USS *Hornet*, so the plan was to have them fly over Japan and ditch in China after bombing Tokyo. While most of the crew would survive the mission, a few died during the raid, all of the planes were lost, and Japanese search parties eventually captured a number of Americans and executed three of them. One of the crews landed in the Soviet Union and would end up being interned there for a year.

From a tactical standpoint, the raid accomplished nothing of note, and Doolittle actually thought he would be punished for the results, but the Doolittle Raid served its purpose of boosting American resolve and demonstrating to the Japanese that they could be attacked at home as well. Furthermore, the Doolittle Raid showed the importance of air power in the war. It helped convince military planners of the power of a strong air force that could not only shift the balance of battles but could also hit military-industrial areas from long-range and thus cripple a nation's war-making abilities. The Japanese would take the capabilities of airplanes into account when formulating how to defend their empire, and it would help compel their leaders to make decisions such as the ones that led to the decisive Battle of Midway later in 1942.

A B-25B *Mitchell* taking off on the raid

For Japan, the mission forced them to come to terms with the fact that the home islands were vulnerable. The fact that sites around the Imperial Palace had been bombed was both shocking and humiliating for the emperor and government officials, and the vulnerability Japanese officials felt caused them to reinforce the home islands, thus diverting resources that otherwise could have been used to expand their territory and engage the Americans' Pacific Fleet. This was especially apparent as Japanese forces pulled back from an attempt on the south Pacific, and especially Australia.

For the United States, the Doolittle Raid showed the nation that they were capable of attacking the Japanese home islands, and also that Japan was a beatable enemy. At the same time, the perceived success of the Doolittle Raid also concerned some military officials who worried that the humiliation the Japanese military most likely felt might compel them to engage in carrier attacks against Hawaii and the West Coast. This forced the military to reinforce these areas, which took away from the Europe-first policy that the Roosevelt administration was engaged in.

In the wake of the raid, the Japanese carriers continued to operate to powerful effect throughout the Pacific. Lacking radar at this stage in the war – in which the IJN lagged behind the Americans disastrously – the Japanese used a naval doctrine intended to keep their adversaries at arm's length: "Because carriers were viewed as highly vulnerable to attack, the essential precondition for carrier combat was that the IJN strike first. This explains the Japanese emphasis on having large carrier air groups composed of aircraft uniformly lighter than their opponents: the larger size of the group and the lighter-weight aircraft gave the Japanese superior striking range." (Stille, 2007. 13).

The Americans tended to use heavier, harder-hitting aircraft with a shorter range. American carriers kept their aircraft complement on deck, using the hangar deck for maintenance and repairs, and launched quickly once battle began. This meant that each American carrier fielded a considerably higher number of aircraft than a Japanese carrier of equivalent size, which, at times, assisted in giving the USN a favorable concentration of force when confronting IJN carrier forces.

Conversely, Japanese strategy, immediately following Pearl Harbor, centered on the newly proven power of concentrating multiple aircraft carriers in a task force, rather than using them in a scattered fashion. The IJN continued to place inordinate value on its gigantic battleships also, but carrier warfare assumed ever-mushrooming importance in operational theory and practice.

The Japanese advance continued during the following months as the Empire's naval and air forces snapped up one island after another. At the start of May 1942, the Japanese planned a complicated push into the Coral Sea off the eastern coast of Australia. As with many Imperial plans, the Japanese seemed to take a curious delight in preparing a strategy so pointlessly labyrinthine that it confused their commanders and squandered any advantages they enjoyed over their adversaries.

In broad outlines, the Japanese forces – with command divided between seven different admirals – would aim for four objectives. The Tulagi Invasion Group would move southeast from Rabaul to take the Solomon Islands, including Tulagi and Guadalcanal, before making a vast movement to the northeast to take Nauru. A second invasion force, the Port Moresby Invasion Group, would head south from Rabaul and sweep around the eastern end of New Guinea to take Port Moresby on the south coast.

Simultaneously, two other forces would advance. One, under Admiral Goto, would strike along the western side of the Solomon Islands to attack the U.S. naval forces in the northern Coral Sea. The other, under Admiral "King Kong" Takagi, victor of the Battle of the Java Sea, would move down the east of the Solomons, then circle northwest to attack the Americans from the south, while also sending aircraft from the aircraft carriers over the Great Barrier Reef to attack the Australian mainland airfields.

The famous American Admiral Chester Nimitz anticipated the Japanese move, though its precise objectives remained unknown to him. While other USN commanders wanted to disperse the four carriers available – *Yorktown, Lexington, Enterprise,* and *Hornet* – around the Coral Sea, Nimitz insisted on concentrating them into a single powerful force swarming with lethal clouds of aircraft. This idea led to the adoption of a superior operational method that gave U.S. naval forces dominance throughout the rest of the Pacific struggle, but it required considerable argument on Nimitz's part to find initial acceptance: "[I]t took Nimitz's forceful lobbying at their San Francisco conference to persuade [Ernest J. King] that now was the time to concentrate the four carriers – sans battleships – into one powerful strategic force. This was a major shift in the way the U.S. Navy viewed its carriers, and it marked Nimitz as exerting aggressive leadership as a theater commander." (Borneman, 2012, 246).

Nimitz

For the coming encounter, the American carriers fell under the command of Vice Admiral William "Bull" Halsey, while Rear Admiral Raymond Spruance led the cruisers and destroyers guarding the quartet of flattops and the oilers providing logistical support. Overall command lay with Rear Admiral Frank Fletcher. From March through early May, the carriers projected

American power and disrupted Japanese operations with their strike aircraft, sinking transports, supply ships, and even the occasional destroyer. These ships also launched the Doolittle Raid.

As the Japanese moved south, carrying out their excessively complex plan, the American carrier group struck back. 40 airplanes based on *Yorktown* attacked IJN forces during their May 4th, 1942 landings on Tulagi in the Solomon Islands. Four ships, three of them small minesweepers and the fourth a destroyer, fell victim to the U.S. pilots.

This small but stinging loss goaded Yamamoto into seeking destruction of the American carriers, which he correctly viewed as the most dangerous piece in play against the Japanese expansion. Three Japanese carriers opened the Battle of the Coral Sea on May 7th, 1942 – the diminutive *Shoho*, carrying 18 aircraft, and the larger *Zuikaku* and *Shokaku* mustering a combined total of 121 airplanes.

134 aircraft, aboard *Yorktown* and *Lexington*, formed the offensive arm of the force sent to intercept the Japanese intrusion into the Coral Sea proper. At 8:15 in the morning on May 7th, American aerial scouts misidentified a pair of Japanese cruisers, accompanied by two destroyers, as Japanese aircraft carriers. Admiral Fletcher ordered 93 bombers and torpedo aircraft into the air.

Shortly thereafter, new scouting reports corrected the earlier error, but Fletcher opted to keep his powerful strike force aloft rather than waste valuable time landing the airplanes on the flattops again. His gamble paid off when reconnaissance aircraft spotted the *Shoho* and radioed its position to Fletcher and the massive flight of American airplanes. Ten minutes before noon, the *Shoho* suffered a devastating one-two punch of bombs and torpedoes which destroyed every aircraft aboard, killed 580 men, and crippled the ship, as an American officer recounted, "VB-2 had been ordered to coordinate their attack with the torpedo attack and this was done in an exceptionally fine manner. [...] The near hits of the 1,000 pound bombs caused billows of black smoke, which formed a very good smoke screen and allowed the torpedo planes to gain an advantageous position before dropping. [...] The observed results were nine torpedo hits on the CV which was the only vessel attacked. The ship was seen to settle slowly and lose speed rapidly. When last seen she was dead in the water." (Stille, 2007, 54).

Gutted by 13 bombs and 7-9 torpedoes, the *Shoho* sank within four minutes of the USN strike. The IJN destroyer *Sazinami* arrived two hours later to pick up the survivors. The exultant Robert E. Dixon of the *Lexington*'s air wing radioed "Scratch one flat top!" That phrase was destined to rank among the most famous quotations of the Pacific War.

The Americans clearly drew "first blood" in the Battle of the Coral Sea, and a Japanese attempt at a counterattack in the evening hours of May 7th failed. The two large fleet carriers sent up 27 aircraft to strike at the American aircraft carrier task force 350 miles west of their position. However, the American fighter screen shot down nine aircraft and forced the rest to return to their carriers, though a few pilots saw the American carriers on the horizon before turning towards home.

The IJN managed to draw some blood on May 7th, however, during the mid to late afternoon. The Japanese forces sank a destroyer, the USS Sims, with three 550-lb bombs delivered by Type 99 dive-bombers, killing or drowning many of the luckless ship's crew. Other bombers damaged the oiler *Neosho*, but temporary repairs enabled the vessel to survive up to its evacuation and scuttling on May 11th, 1942.

A picture of the damaged *Neosho*

If the first day provided triumphs mostly to the Americans, the second day witnessed more of a draw between the two sides. Between 8 and 9 A.M. on May 8th, the Americans and Japanese successfully located one another. The USN scrambled its aircraft first, yet due to encountering a squall, the airplanes only inflicted light damage on a single Japanese carrier, the *Shokaku*. The Japanese dive-bombers and torpedo bombers inflicted considerably more damage on the *Yorktown* and *Lexington,* despite suffering heavy aircraft losses. Shimazaki Shigekazu described the whirling chaos of battle: "When we attacked the enemy carriers we ran into a virtual wall of antiaircraft fire; the carriers and their supporting ships blackened the sky with exploding shells and tracers. It seemed impossible that we could survive out bombing and torpedo runs through such incredible defenses. Our Zeros and enemy Wildcats spun, dove, and climbed in the midst of our formations. Burning and shattered planes of both sides plunged from the skies." (Stille, 2007, 56).

Both *Yorktown* and *Lexington* suffered damage during the attacks. The *Yorktown* eventually returned to the United States for repairs, but the *Lexington* suffered internal explosions shortly before 1 PM due to combustion of leaking fuel vapors. The aircraft carrier sank as a result, with 2,735 men evacuated and 216 killed at various times during the initial strikes and later during the unexpected explosions.

Pictures of the *Lexington* under attack during the battle

The Battle of the Coral Sea ended with neither force capable of continuing the fight. However, the Americans halted the Japanese advance and ended the IJN's string of victories, revealing the surprising weaknesses under the veneer of Imperial Japanese invincibility. From this point on, the naval war led to the steady destruction of Japanese naval and air forces as the Americans rolled inexorably westward across the Pacific.

Chapter 6: Midway

By the time of the Coral Sea engagement, Admiral Yamamoto, Commander of the Japanese Combined Fleet, had won his own political battle; his view that the priority in the Pacific should be the American fleet had finally prevailed. The fact that American carrier-borne bombers had hit Tokyo in April during the famous Doolittle Raid had helped him. Though militarily insignificant, the raid had nonetheless badly shaken Japanese national pride. By the time Japan's military leaders were on board with Yamamoto's intentions of striking the American fleet, Yamamoto had conceived a bold plan for drawing these units out into a pitched battle. He knew that the Americans, now fighting a naval war in two oceans, were nervous about exposing their precious carriers. Another lunge towards Pearl Harbor would surely force them to fight, but the strong garrison and numerous aircraft now based on Hawaii made this too risky. Instead, Yamamoto would threaten Midway, the tiny island base which represented America's most western toehold. Midway lies about 1,200 miles directly west of the Hawaiian islands, and about 2,300 miles east of Japan. Thus, "Operation MI" was born.

Midway in November 1941

The plan was to use a carrier strike force to bomb the island, with a separate invasion fleet putting troops ashore in the aftermath. Both would be supported by the main Japanese battle fleet, again operating separately. Meanwhile, another force including two light carriers would strike north towards the American held Aleutian islands ("Operation AL"). Given the damage done at Coral Sea and the decision to send two carriers north, Yamamoto only had four fleet carriers and two light carriers for the Midway operation, but he also knew that the *Lexington* had been sunk and suspected that the *Yorktown* would be in dry dock for months. Assuming that the Americans would keep at least two carriers in the Atlantic, Yamamoto thought his fleet was big enough, and in terms of the raw numbers, this was a reasonable judgment to make at the time.

Unbeknownst to the Japanese, the main disadvantage Japan would have at Midway was the fact the U.S. could read their radio traffic. With the success of their codebreakers, Americans were able to understand Japan's communications in the Pacific in the days leading up to the battle, and even when the routine issue of new Japanese code books meant that the Americans were once again in the dark, analysts working for the Navy in Hawaii were reasonably confident that as the Japanese units left port, Midway was their target and June 4 would be the date of their arrival. This intelligence was enough to allow Admiral Chester Nimitz, the commander of the Pacific Fleet, to prepare an ambush.

Although Nimitz had strong intelligence, he also had to be very mindful of the limitations of his own forces. The two key indices of naval power in 1942 were the battleship and the aircraft carrier, and even though modern writers are apt to point out that the days of the former were numbered (since the aircraft carrier could deliver its punch before a battleship could get anywhere near close enough to engage it), this was still a period of transition. Carrier operations at night remained a highly risky proposition, leaving open the possibility that battleships might be able to close the range under cover of darkness. At the same time, carriers were highly vulnerable to submarine attacks.

In the summer of 1942, Nimitz had plenty of issues to deal with. Most of the American battleships were either sunk at their moorings in Pearl Harbor, supporting the British in the Atlantic, or back in San Francisco, so Nimitz had an unbalanced fleet in Hawaii. He had to ensure that the American carriers did not get caught by the powerful Japanese battleships, and he also had to make sure the American carriers could win the action against Japan's own carriers.

Nimitz had two carriers in Task Force (TF) 16: the *Enterprise* and the *Hornet*. He also had a third, the *Yorktown*, in TF 17. *Yorktown* had been rushed to Pearl Harbor for emergency repairs after the battle of the Coral Sea, but in an astonishing feat of teamwork and repairs, she was patched up in time to sortie just 72 hours later. These two Task Forces were escorted by heavy cruisers and destroyers, and operating separately were several flotillas of submarines, as well as land-based aircraft flying out of Midway. The Midway air base had been reinforced from Hawaii on the basis of the new intelligence.

The USS *Enterprise*

The USS *Hornet*

While the Americans were moving into position, the Japanese were surging westwards towards Midway. In the lead was Admiral Nagumo with his carrier group, the 1st Kido Butai (Mobile Force). It consisted of four carriers - the *Kaga, Akagi, Hiryu* and *Soryu* - with plenty of escorts, including two battleships and two heavy cruisers. Nagumo reported to Admiral Yamamoto, architect of the attack on Pearl Harbor and Commander in Chief of the Nihon Kigun (Imperial Japanese Navy).

Nagumo

Yamamoto was a long way behind Nagumo, aboard the *Yamato*, and his was the main battle fleet, including three battleships and the light carrier *Hosho*. There was also the Midway invasion force, which consisted of two battleships, another light carrier, and the troop transports. Each force was supplemented by destroyers, light cruisers, tankers and other logistical vessels. Therefore, they were all powerful mixed surface groups, with the overwhelming bulk of the aircraft in Nagumo's command. This was necessary because the Japanese task forces were not close enough to each other to offer realistic support in the event of a fight, meaning they were all essentially operating as independent units.

As dusk fell on June 2, the Americans knew the Japanese planned a major offensive towards Midway that would undoubtedly include carriers and battleships, but they had little inkling of the makeup or deployment of the force beyond that. Early histories have often overstated the degree of intelligence detail available to the Americans at this stage. Fletcher rightly expected the Japanese carriers to be split into two strike forces, and that they would approach from the west or north, but he would later need to respond to a single carrier group approaching from the southwest. For their part, the Japanese knew that the American heavy units were not at Pearl

Harbor, but it seems likely that Nagumo was not given specific confirmation of this. Yamamoto knew about it back with the main force, but his concerns about communicating via radio kept him from tipping off his deputy. As such, the plan for an initial strike against Midway by the carriers went ahead.

At just after 6:00 on the morning of June 4, Fletcher's carriers got word of the Japanese carrier group, and as more details came in, general quarters were sounded and aircrews donned their flight gear, rushing to the briefing rooms to learn about the missions ahead. By the time the Americans launched their strikes, Spruance's TF 16, including the *Hornet* and *Enterprise*, was about 30 miles south of Fletcher's TF 17, which included the *Yorktown*. At 6:07, Spruance had been ordered south and authorized to attack the Japanese carriers as soon as they were firmly located. Fletcher lingered to the north with the *Yorktown* in order to recover his patrol aircraft, which were searching in that direction for what he believed was a second Japanese carrier group.

The launch arrangements for the American carriers, the conduct of their air groups, and the associated navigational and command issues continue to cause controversy, and even today, over 70 years after the battle, a number of important matters remain open to question. What seems to have been lacking was a firm command grip on the overall American effort. Nimitz had rightly called for caution in the use of his carriers and identified a broad plan to capitalize on the American intelligence advantage by deploying to the north of Midway, waiting until the Japanese had committed their planes to an attack on the island, and then launching an all-out assault on the carriers. But coordinating such a plan from Hawaii was impractical, so he had left it to Fletcher and Spruance to firm up on the details, depending on the tactical situation.

Fletcher was the senior Rear Admiral at sea with the fleet, but he was some way to the north, coordinating a peripheral and ultimately fruitless search for a phantom second Japanese carrier group. Thus, the main offensive effort against the already identified Kido Butai was initially left to Spruance and the two carriers of TF 16. They were to rely heavily on the aviation experts sailing with them on the carriers, but even within TF 16 itself, although both *Enterprise* and *Hornet* were ordered to launch strikes, they were permitted to do so independently of each other. To their north, the *Yorktown* was eventually to change course and launch a strike of her own. In essence, the Americans would end up launching three entirely separate air attacks on Nagumo's fleet, and any notion of coordination over the target among the three carriers would therefore be a sheer matter of luck. If the five brave but disorganized attacks from Midway, which had already been comprehensively defeated by the Japanese, were any indication, this was a recipe for disaster.

The men launching their attack from the *Hornet* had perhaps the most miserable story to recount. With a total of 76 aircraft available for the attack, on paper the *Hornet* had the most firepower of the three carriers, and the aircraft were led by Commander Stanhope Ring, a highly experienced naval aviator, albeit one with little actual combat experience (like most of those at Midway).

Ring

Unfortunately for Ring and his crew, their actual combat experience was greatly lacking in comparison to their Japanese counterparts. Ring's aircraft began to lift off from *Hornet* at about 7:00 on June 4, but they were not actually ready to depart for another hour; it took that long just for each aircraft to take off, circle and take position within Ring's formation. By contrast, the Japanese were able to achieve this in less than 10 minutes with over 100 aircraft. Compounding the problem, the estimated range to the target was in excess of 100 miles, already a stretch for the shorter-ranged American aircraft. They could hardly afford to waste fuel circling the carrier for an hour.

As if that wasn't enough, the precise heading taken by Ring's force when it did depart is still the subject of debate, but whatever the case, Lt. Commander John C. Waldron, the leader of Ring's torpedo squadron, was unhappy. In fact, he was so unhappy with the plan that after just 50 miles out from the *Hornet*, Waldron ordered his aircraft to peel off to the right and take a completely different course, not only openly disobeying his commander's instructions but even breaking radio silence in order to do so. His loyal squadron followed him.

Despite now missing half of his bombers in formation, Ring kept his course, but by 9:30 he had yet to sight a single Japanese ship. He then decided to turn south towards Midway, where he hoped to spot Nagumo's Kido Butai, but at that point, Ring's fighter escort, low on fuel, abandoned him and turned back towards the *Hornet*. Ultimately, Ring and the remaining dive bombers eventually landed at Midway itself, but nearly all of the fighters failed to make it back to the *Hornet*, forcing most to ditch into the sea in hopes of being rescued. Very few would.

While Ring was in the middle of a debacle, Waldron's torpedo bombers, which had peeled away from the rest of the group early on, did find the Japanese fleet. He had been right in his navigational judgment (if completely insubordinate in his behaviour), and his aircraft would be the only ones from Hornet to attack the Japanese fleet that morning. Of course, without the rest of Ring's aircrew, they proved to be sitting ducks. At about 9:00, Waldron's 15 Devastators skimmed in towards the Japanese carriers at a sedate 120 mph, in a macabre naval version of the Charge of the Light Brigade. The waiting Zeros pounced, and Waldron's squadron was wiped out by them and the concentrated flak. Of the 30 crew involved, only Ensign George Gay would survive, clinging to a piece of wreckage from his plane. It was brave, it was costly and it was completely ineffective; of the several torpedoes launched, apparently no hits at all were scored[1]. By 9:30, the sky above the Japanese aircraft carriers was clear of enemy planes, while the Japanese planes returning from the Midway attack had safely landed. On board, the crews frantically worked to stow the returning planes, maintain the rotating fighter patrol, and prepare an anti-shipping raid to hit the American carriers.

---

[1] There are those that contest this, claiming some damage was inflicted.

Ensign Gay (right) posing with one of his plane's rear gunners before the attack on June 4.

The lull in the fighting would not last long, because after just past 10:00, Nagumo's carriers began enduring sustained attacks from the *Yorktown* and the *Enterprise* air groups. The following 30 minutes would turn the tide in the Pacific. The *Enterprise*'s air group had finally pulled away from the ship at about 7:45, but even before they did so, their own escorting fighter squadron had disappeared, mistakenly chasing after planes from the distant *Yorktown*. In addition, the slower torpedo bombers got away a full 11 minutes after the Dauntless dive bombers, so this was hardly a compact and well balanced air wing as it made its way toward the Japanese fleet. These were not good omens, but the bombers from the *Enterprise* pressed on unescorted nonetheless.

TBD-1 Devastators on the deck of the *Enterprise* getting ready to take off on June 4

By 9:30, they had still not spotted the Japanese carriers, and matters were now critical in terms of fuel. Unbeknownst to the American planners, Nagumo had changed direction. He had landed all of his returning planes, and now aware of the American carriers, had turned his force to a northeasterly heading. Thus, the Japanese carriers were not where they should have been.

Ultimately, luck and a shrewd command decision worked in the Americans' favor. Lt. Commander Eade McClusky, leading the air group, spotted a lone Japanese destroyer travelling northeast at high speed and guessed (correctly) that it might be returning to the main force after having been detached for some earlier duty. Sure enough, that destroyer had been chasing an American submarine, the *Nautilus*, which had managed to penetrate and discomfort the Japanese destroyer picket earlier in the morning. One of the fleet's older subs, *Nautilus* had picked up a message from a patrolling flying boat at about 4:30 a.m. identifying the approximate location of Nagumo's fleet. Making as good a speed as possible, *Nautilus* managed to slip into the middle of the Japanese formation and fired a salvo of torpedoes at one of the battleships around 8:00, shortly after the first unsuccessful American air attacks from Midway. *Nautilus* then stalked a carrier (probably the *Soryu*) before firing again, this time at a light cruiser. Throughout this adventure, the *Nautilus* was chased and attacked by aircraft and destroyers, so much so that it had to withdraw. All of the submarine's torpedoes misfired or missed, as was usually the case with the U.S. Mark XIV, but the destroyer which was tasked to hang back from the fleet and hunt down the *Nautilus* was the *Arashi*. *Arashi* was ultimately unsuccessful in that mission, and it was this same destroyer which was spotted by McClusky. By following the destroyer, McClusky's air group was effectively vectored straight to Nagumo's fleet, which they sighted some half an hour later. Nimitz would later state that McClusky's decision "decided the fate of our carrier task force and our forces at Midway..."

Meanwhile, the *Yorktown*, dashing south to rejoin Spruance's carriers, launched her own raid at about 9:00, but after a last minute change of plan, one squadron of Dauntless dive bombers and most of the fighters remained aboard the carrier. Still suspecting a second Japanese carrier force (his intelligence had so far only confirmed two cruisers with Nagumo), Fletcher was being cautious, leaving his attacking air group with only six escort fighters. Furthermore, like the planes from the *Enterprise*, the attacking squadrons were strung out rather than concentrated. But as fate would have it, the planes from the *Yorktown* did not experience the navigational difficulties which bedevilled those from TF 16's carriers, because updated intelligence enabled them to fly straight to the target, which they sighted at 10:10.

Thus, just after 10:00 that morning, by luck rather than good judgment, the Americans had managed to assemble three squadrons of dive bombers and two squadrons of torpedo bombers over the Japanese carrier fleet at roughly the same time. The slow torpedo bombers, as they had been all day, were the target of most of the Japanese fighter opposition, due mostly to their potential for damaging ships, as a successful torpedo hit was far more lethal to a carrier or battleship than a bomb strike was likely to be. Thus, it may have been a tactical choice. On the other hand, the Japanese had sufficient fighters to do both jobs, with at least 30 and probably 40 in the air at any given moment. Most of these stayed at low level and attacked the torpedo bombers, and some took on the dive bombers as they came down to release their bombs, but in most cases this was after they had done so and were on their way back up. In other words, there were no fighters allocated to engage the dive bombers as they approached the fleet at higher altitude. This points to another problem the Japanese had: coordination of their immediate fleet's defense was difficult. Unlike the Americans, they had no radar and therefore relied on visual contact for the identification of intruders. Second, their radio equipment was poor and often ignored by the pilots. Third, the fighter pilots, while highly skilled, were imbued with bushido, the Japanese martial tradition that emphasised individual aggression rather than teamwork.

None of this was good news for the torpedo bombers that attacked the *Kaga* and *Soryu*. Of the two attacks, the attack by the planes of the *Enterprise* against the *Kaga* was the more sophisticated. The 14 aircraft came at the *Kaga* from two directions in a textbook pincer attack, but of the eight torpedoes dropped; all of them missed. The price was again high, with 9 of the aircraft being shot down. Of the 12 torpedo planes from *Yorktown* that attacked the *Soryu*, only four were to survive. Hits were claimed, but the carrier emerged unscathed yet again. The American torpedo attacks at Midway were therefore an expensive failure. No damage was done to the Japanese fleet, and dozens of Americans were killed. It now seems possible that some of the torpedoes may have hit their targets but failed to detonate, since the American Mark XIV torpedo used at the time was hopelessly unreliable.

In one sense though, the attacks did serve a useful purpose by keeping the Japanese fighters off the dive bombers. The Dauntless dive bombers, consisting of two squadrons from *Enterprise* and one from *Yorktown*[2], were a new type optimized for this specialist role, and on this occasion they employed it, eschewing the easier glide bombing technique used earlier in the day by the Marines from Midway. The steeper angle of a true dive bombing run (about 70 degrees) was far less vulnerable to flak and far more accurate. Japanese carriers had thin unarmored flight decks, and on board the ships there were hundreds of aircraft, many of them being refuelled and re-armed. All the factors were now aligned for a devastating attack.

Yorktown's VB3 dive bombing squadron hit the *Soryu* just as *Yorktown's* torpedo bombers had made their unsuccessful run in at wave-skimming altitude. The VB3s dropped out of the sky right on top of the ship, like sinister birds of prey, and at least five hits punched through the *Soryu's* flight deck, immediately causing devastating fires and mass casualties. Additional near misses sent huge shockwaves ringing through the hull. Soryu was doomed.

---

[2] Yorktown's second Dauntless squadron remained on board in reserve.

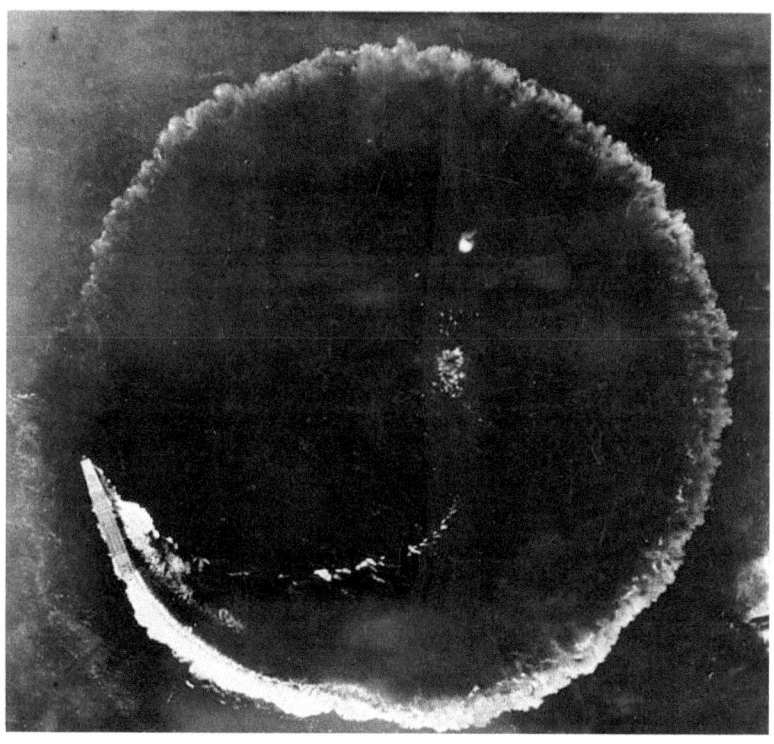

Aerial photo of *Soryu* earlier on June 4

The fate of *Kaga* and *Akagi* would be similar. In the confusion of combat, most of the attack by the crews of the *Enterprise* went in against the *Kaga*, which suffered at least five direct hits and was soon ablaze from bow to stern. *Nautilus*, the only submarine to make any significant contribution to the battle, returned to the scene during the mid-afternoon and fired three torpedoes at the crippled Kaga, but once again, the submarine was let down by faulty ordnance. One torpedo hit the carrier and failed to explode. Meanwhile, the *Akagi*, despite only being attacked by one section of VB-6s, took two direct hits that started fires on board, and a near miss off the stern jammed the rudder over, making all attempts to steer the ship impossible.

The men of *Enterprise's* VB-6s

Within 10 minutes, the entire complexion of the battle had changed. Three of Nagumo's carriers had been crippled, leaving only the *Hiryu* undamaged. Carrier doctrine had long emphasised the importance of getting in the first blow, and even though it took so many attempts to land such a blow, Nimitz's three carriers nonetheless remained completely unscathed, while three of Nagumo's were on fire.

A Navy diorama depicting the damage they believed they had inflicted on the Japanese on June 4. The diorama depicts the *Soryu* (center foreground), *Kaga* and *Akagi* (both in the center background) all burning.

Although they did not yet know it for certain, the Americans had wiped out the Japanese offensive air arm with the loss of only one carrier, but that did not mean the battle was over. Later on the evening of June 4, aircraft from the two surviving American carriers again set out to attack the Kido Butai, in the belief that there might be a fifth Japanese carrier. As dusk fell, they failed to find anything but wreckage, and the subsequent night landings only caused confusion and additional casualties. That same night, the American submarine *Tambor* encountered a force of four Japanese cruisers. These had been detached by Nagumo to bombard Midway in preparation for the intended amphibious assault, but after being called back to the rest of the fleet, they saw the *Tambor*'s periscope and took evasive action. During these maneuvers, two of the cruisers collided, suffering substantial damage. As the submarine withdrew, the two damaged cruisers were left behind by their compatriots to make as best a speed as they could.

The dawn of June 5 found TF 16 heading south, then northwest, in a hunt for a phantom fifth Japanese carrier. Meanwhile, Yamamoto and Nagumo were still hoping to concentrate their forces and entice the American carriers westwards. If they could achieve that, they might be able to bring on a close range night action or move the battle within range of their land-based aircraft on the island of Wake.

However, the main forces of both sides did not establish contact with each other throughout the day. Instead, the action would focus on the two damaged Japanese cruisers, which were now joined by an anti-submarine escort of two destroyers. This latter precaution would actually prove unnecessary, because in one of the more peculiar decisions of the battle, the American submarine commander had already ordered all of his subs to pull back.

However, the damaged cruisers had left a highly visible fuel slick on the surface of the ocean, making it easy for an aircraft to follow, and they were also less than 100 miles from Midway itself. Thus, it was not long before they came under attack by American land-based bombers. There were three such assaults, starting at about 7:00. The first two were pressed home by the Marines, who were flying their elderly Vindicator dive bombers yet again, but this time there were no Japanese Zeros to counter them. Nevertheless, the anti-aircraft flak screen was intense. Although some damage and casualties were inflicted on the cruisers, these attacks were unlikely to sink such well-protected vessels. The much circulated story of one of the Vindicators intentionally nose-diving into a cruiser in a kamikaze-like "suicide" appears to be a myth; the plane had been shot down and crashed close by the ship. Once again, brave Marine aviators had taken significant losses for little in return. They were followed by the even less successful air force heavies, flying in at 20,000 feet and predictably dropping their bombs harmlessly into the ocean. After the attacks, the two cruisers and their escorts continued limping back toward the rest of the Japanese fleet.

Further north, Spruance's two carriers launched their own strike later that afternoon after a suspected contact with the Japanese about 250 miles northwest. There were heated arguments on board the *Enterprise* about the tactics to be employed, because this would be a long reach for the Dauntless bombers even if the carriers sailed after them in the same direction at full speed. Bomb loads were eventually reduced, and the launch was delayed, all in an effort to ensure the attackers could return safely to the carriers. Ultimately, 58 aircraft took off and set off in a fruitless search for another Japanese aircraft carrier. Unable to find the nonexistent carrier, they settled on attacking the *Tanikaze*, but they did not heavily damage that maneuverable Japanese destroyer.

June 6 was the last day of active combat in the three day mini-campaign that became known as the Battle of Midway. Early that morning, the *Hornet* launched a dive bomber mission, with fighter escort, against the two damaged Japanese cruisers. About two hours behind the *Hornet's* aircraft came those from the *Enterprise*, again escorted by fighters. Ironically, these two waves enjoyed more fighter support than had been available to the bombers that had taken on the full might of the Kido Butai only two days earlier. Of course, the escort fighters had no Zeros to worry about this time, and despite a heroic defense, the two cruisers and one of the escorting destroyers were badly hit by the dive bombers. Eventually, the fire on board one of the cruisers reached the torpedoes stored on deck, causing a large explosion and sinking the cruiser a few hours later. In an episode characteristic of the U.S. tactical intelligence effort during Midway, the attacks on this modest force had repeatedly been reported as being against one or two "battleships". It was only later in the evening that aerial photography confirmed the sunken vessel had been the heavy cruiser *Mikuma*, with her damaged sister ship *Mogami* getting away. The brave defense of this little force over two days, and the fact that three out of the four ships eventually made it back to port, stands testimony to the professionalism and abilities of the Imperial Japanese Navy.

The damaged *Mikuma*

The final chapter of the Battle of Midway exemplified the difficulties of even finding and identifying the enemy. Despite the fact there had been heavy engagements the previous two days, a force of B-17 Flying Fortresses managed to bomb an American submarine during the afternoon of June 6, mistaking it for a Japanese heavy cruiser.

Ironically, the last aircraft carrier to sink as a result of the Battle of Midway was an American one. By the early afternoon on June 6, there was some optimism about the prospect of saving the *Yorktown*, as salvage crews had put out the fires and stabilised the vessel using pumps. The *Yorktown* was also surrounded by 6 protective destroyers as an escort. However, these destroyers failed to detect the Japanese submarine I-168, which crept to within easy torpedo range. In the middle of the afternoon on June 6, the submarine fired four torpedoes, two of which punched through the *Yorktown's* hull, causing more extensive flooding. The third hit the destroyer *Hammann*, sinking the destroyer within three minutes and causing mass casualties. The fourth torpedo missed, and the I168 was chased off by the remaining American destroyers. Abandoned yet again, the heavily listing *Yorktown* eventually slipped beneath the waves at 5:00 the following morning.

Picture of the Hammann sinking

The Battle of Midway was one of the first major naval battles in history where the enemy fleets never actually saw or came into contact with each other, and by the time the battle was over, the Japanese defeat was so devastating that it was actually kept secret from all but the highest echelons of the Japanese government. Along with the loss of hundreds of aircraft and over 3,000 men killed, the four Japanese aircraft carriers lost, when compared to America's one lost carrier, was critical considering America's huge shipbuilding superiority. American shipbuilding would prove more than able to do the rest, and henceforth, it would be difficult for Japan to challenge America's might in the field of carrier warfare. The U.S. still lagged behind in terms of battleships and tactical competence in "old fashioned" surface actions, but the Guadalcanal campaign would give the Americans plenty of experience as well.

Perhaps the most ironic aspect of the Battle of Midway is that the battle, which would prove so decisive in terms of the outcome in the Pacific, was neither a positional nor territorial battle. Midway was merely a convenient target chosen by Yamamoto to draw the Americans out, and both sides' objectives were attritional attempts to degrade their opponents' carrier units. Nevertheless, the result created space for the Americans to begin their cautious advance back across the Pacific. This started with Guadalcanal and proceeded along two axes. Nimitz would command the larger and predominantly naval effort across the central Pacific, and island fortresses such as Saipan and Iwo Jima would soon go down in military legend. To the south, General Douglas MacArthur led a campaign across New Guinea and the Philippines, with a more land-based focus. Notwithstanding that, it was off Leyte Gulf in the Philippines in October 1944 that the Imperial Japanese Navy suffered a fatal blow in the largest naval battle in history, during which four carriers and three battleships were lost. Japan's Southern Resource Zone was thus collapsed from two different directions, and by early 1945, with the fall of Manila and Okinawa, the end was clearly in sight.

The end result of the Battle of Midway is well-known, but many of the critical details of the fighting itself are often glossed over, and in a sense that does a disservice to the Americans who won the battle. Today, it's often forgotten that Japan had critical advantages in both numbers and combat experience. Japan undoubtedly had more experienced aircrew and supporting maintenance staff; the ability of the Japanese to assemble their strike forces so much faster is testimony to this, and it very well could have had a consequential impact on the battle itself. The sailors and airmen aboard the Japanese carriers were seen as elite, and they had struck the first blow at Pearl Harbor. Many had fought for years in China.

Japan also had the better aircraft. The Kate torpedo bombers outclassed the American Vindicators and even the brand new Avenger in every respect. The Zero fighters were also in a different league. Furthermore, all of the aircraft on Japan's carriers outranged the American equivalents by quite a margin, and Japan's ships were state of the art, fast and extremely well armed.

As if that wasn't enough of an advantage, Japan had a distinct advantage in numbers, with four carriers against three, and a monopoly of battleships. It was only in the area of land-based aircraft on Midway that the U.S. had an advantage, but the attacks made by those planes early on June 4 did not help much at all.

Chapter 7: Japan's Last Gasp

Following the decisive American victory at Midway, the Americans began their "island-hopping campaign" to conquer and bring the Japanese to bay on their home islands. The Navy provided the heavy lifting through this entire struggle, transporting troops and supplies, giving shore support with carrier aircraft raids and heavy bombardments from battleship, cruiser, and destroyer guns used as artillery, and defeating concentrations of IJN ships and aircraft wherever found.

The Guadalcanal Campaign, which ran from August 1942 to February 1943, was a bitter and protracted struggle that also happened to be a strange and transitional confrontation quite unlike any other in the long Pacific War. In conjunction with the American victory at the Battle of

Midway, Guadalcanal represented the crucial moment when the balance of power in the Pacific tipped in favor of the Allies, but the idea that Guadalcanal would be such a significant battle would have come as a surprise to military strategists and planners on both sides.

Nonetheless, by the time the Guadalcanal campaign was underway, it was a confrontation that neither side actively sought, but that both sides came to believe they could not afford to lose. When Allied forces landed on the island, it was an effort to deny the Japanese the use of the island and other nearby islands, but the Japanese defenders fought bitterly in an effort to push them off the island, resulting in a rather unique battle that consisted mostly of a Japanese offensive against Americans that invaded amphibiously and dug in. While the Americans closed the campaign with a substantial material advantage, the American garrison on Guadalcanal was initially undermanned and terribly undersupplied.

Eventually, nearly 100,000 soldiers fought on the island, and the ferocity with which the Japanese fought was a fitting prelude to campaigns like Iwo Jima and Okinawa. The campaign would include six separate naval battles, three large-scale land clashes, and almost daily skirmishing and shelling. Not surprisingly, the campaign exacted a heavy toll, with more than 60 ships sunk, more than 1200 aircraft destroyed, and more than 38,000 dead. While the Japanese and Americans engaged at sea and in the skies, of the 36,000 Japanese defenders on the ground, over 30,000 of them would be dead by the end of the Guadalcanal campaign, while the Americans lost about 7,000 killed.

By the end of the fighting, the Guadalcanal Campaign had unquestionably become a turning point in the Pacific War, representing both the last gasp of the Japanese offensive and the first stirrings of the American onslaught. In the wake of the Japanese defeat, Major General Kiyotake Kawaguchi asserted, "Guadalcanal is no longer merely a name of an island in Japanese military history. It is the name of the graveyard of the Japanese army."

The Battle of the Philippine Sea, also known as the "Great Marianas Turkey Shoot," occurred on June 19th and 20th, 1944 during the Americans' approach to the Philippines. During this battle, 7 American fleet carriers and 8 light carriers under Admirals Spruance and Mitscher squared off against the IJN's 5 fleet carriers and 4 light carriers, plus air assets based on Guam. On the first day, the F6F Hellcats and other American aircraft butchered the Japanese Zero fighters and other aircraft, downing 550 to 650 with minimal losses on their own side.

The second day of the "Turkey Shoot" witnessed American attacks on the Japanese fleet proper, sinking three fleet carriers though at the cost of over 100 aircraft. Many of these casualties resulted from the American pilots running out of fuel after their long attack runs, as well as nightfall catching many far from their home carriers: "[T]he return trip home became a nightmare for many pilots as they attempted to stretch their limited fuel supplies in a vain attempt to find friendly carriers in the darkness. Many ditched in the ocean, some in silence, others after sad, dramatic farewells over the radio; many finally saw the task force in the distance, as Mitscher issued his courageous order to "Turn on the lights." [...] Extensive rescue operations the next day resulted in a final tally of 16 pilots and 33 air crewmen lost during the day's action." (Wooldridge, 1993, 134).

Though most of the Japanese carriers escaped, hundreds of Japan's most skilled and experienced pilots died in the skies or the waters of the Philippine Sea. Though the Japanese replaced the lost aircraft in time, the pilots represented an asset the Empire found itself incapable of replacing before the war's end.

The last major naval action of the Pacific War occurred at the Battle of Leyte Gulf, which was the largest naval battle of the war and possibly the largest in history. As the Americans closed in on Leyte, the Imperial Japanese Navy made a final effort to engage and defeat the massed naval forces of their inexorable enemy. Approaching from multiple directions, the IJN's force failed to coordinate properly, while the Americans, benefitting from excellent communications and scouting, held and exploited a strong tactical advantage.

Pounded by torpedoes from submarines and destroyers, mauled by the heavy guns of American cruisers and battleships, and savaged by the omnipresent clouds of American dive-bombers, torpedo bombers, and rocket-equipped fighters, the Japanese lost 45% of their tonnage, 10 tons of ships for every 1 ton lost by the Americans during the battle. Worse yet, the U.S. forces represented only a bit of the total naval might the Navy had at its disposal, while the Japanese committed almost all their remaining ships to the battle. A later interview highlighted the combat's significance: "'Would you say that, to all intents and purposes, the naval war ended with the battle of October?' Admiral Ozawa was asked. 'After this battle,' replied the Japanese Admiral, 'the surface forces became strictly auxiliary, so that we relied on land forces, special [Kamikaze] attack, and air power.' He added this significant obituary: 'There was no further use assigned to surface vessels, with exception of some special ships.' Viewed in this light, Leyte Gulf becomes more than a victorious battle or a successful campaign. In many ways it was the death struggle of the Japanese Navy." (Woodward, 2007, 162-163).

Both *Musashi* and *Yamato* served in the Battle of Leyte Gulf. On October 24th, 1944, the *Musashi* came under heavy attack over the course of several hours from aircraft originating mainly on the *Lexington* and *Essex*. Its decks strafed by F6F Hellcats and bombed by Curtiss SB2C Helldiver dive-bombers, and its sides pounded by torpedoes dropped by Grumman TBF Avenger torpedo bombers, the *Musashi* continued across the Sibuyan Sea in support of other Japanese vessels, and even managed to shoot down some of its tormentors.

A picture of the *Musashi* under attack

Temporarily abandoned by the other ships in the afternoon, the *Musashi* steadily took on vast quantities of water despite frantic efforts to prevent the vessel's loss. As the ship's list increased fatally, other Japanese vessels managed to evacuate slightly more than half of its crew complement, plus most of the survivors of the *Maya*, whom the *Musashi* rescued earlier in the day. The vessel capsized and sank at 7:36 PM, taking its captain to the depths with it, after at least 19 torpedoes punctured its hull during the day.

Paul Allen, one of the founding partners of Microsoft, located the *Musashi's* remains in 3,300 feet of water in 2015 by utilizing a remote-controlled undersea vehicle. The *Musashi* apparently detonated while sinking and might have exploded even if it remained at the surface, indicating serious internal damage from the American strikes: "Though the failing warship disappeared under the water in one piece, it apparently exploded once underwater, as pieces of the ship are strewn across the ocean floor. Amid the debris, the footage revealed a mount for the seal of the Imperial Japanese Navy, a chrysanthemum made out of teak, which had rotted away over seven decades on the ocean floor." (Pruitt, 2015, 1).

The *Yamato* suffered only seven bomb strikes during the Battle of Leyte Gulf and retired mostly intact following the Japanese defeat. The battleship fired at an American aircraft carrier at a range of 20 miles but failed to score any hits, despite its crew's claims to the contrary. This represented the sole occasion on which the *Yamato's* guns fired upon an enemy vessel, underlining the profound uselessness of "super battleships" in 1944.

The *Yamato's* terminal deployment occurred when the ship sallied to attack American vessels supporting landings on Okinawa in 1945. The giant ship suffered a grim and futile end: "The small force was tracked by submarines and aircraft and on the following day, over 400 carrier aircraft attacked the fleet. In no case did a bomb penetrate *Yamato's* armored deck, but no ship could withstand the pounding of torpedoes that the Americans concentrated on her port side. [...] Hit by as many as 11 or 13 torpedoes [...] *Yamato* rolled over to port. An explosion of her aft magazines left a huge plume of smoke visible in Kyushu, over 100 miles away, and marked the end of the Imperial Navy." (Stille, 2008, 43).

3,063 Japanese died and 269 survived, in exchange for a mere 12 American lives lost among the attacking air crews. Huge, almost (but not quite) indestructible, and armed with vast quantities of ordnance that never came within range of an enemy ship to pulverize, the *Yamato*-class battleships forcefully underlined the passing of an earlier era when such vessels ruled the seas, and the irreversible assumption of predominance by the aircraft carrier and the strike aircraft it supported.

As evidence of just how desperate the Japanese were by this time, the first organized, large-scale use of kamikaze tactics came during the battle of Leyte Gulf. In October 1944, the Imperial Japanese Navy, and particularly its Air Service, was a shadow of its former self. In 1941, at the outset of the Pacific War, Japanese naval aviation was arguably the most formidable in the world; its pilots were the best-trained, its aircraft were the most technologically advanced, and its leadership was the most tactically sophisticated. Even in June 1942, the American Navy entered the decisive Battle of Midway at a distinct disadvantage, and luck and cunning, not superior technology or overwhelming force, won Midway for the Americans. From that point forward, however, as the United States began to exploit more fully its vast human and material resources, and as the conflict evolved into a grinding war of attrition of the sort that Japan was not suited to wage, Japan's capacity to prosecute an air war against America declined precipitously. In June 1944, at the Battle of the Philippine Sea, with three fleet carriers sunk and perhaps 600 aircraft lost, the remnant of Japan's Naval Air Service was decisively crushed.

As the U.S. forces steadily moved closer to Japan, the Japanese had neither the aircraft nor the trained pilots needed to mount carrier-based operations. Facing this dilemma, and called upon to stage a last-ditch defense of Japan's empire against the oncoming American advance, the Naval Air Service sought out a radical change in tactics. In fact, the desperate situation of Japanese aviators on and around the Philippines had already driven several to adopt haphazard kamikaze attacks. There were two unsuccessful attempts at suicide attacks on September 13, 1944, and another on October 15. On October 21, the same day that the first organized kamikaze strike took off from Luzon, a single Japanese aircraft, likely either an Aichi D3A dive-bomber or a Mitsubishi Ki-51, seemed to crash deliberately into the *HMAS Australia*, an Australian heavy cruiser, killing 30, wounding 64, and causing major damage. The unknown pilot apparently acted on his own initiative, and his attack was not part of an organized kamikaze strike.

Having lost the vast majority of its experienced flyers, and with demand for pilots higher than ever before, the Japanese Navy had no choice but to rush new recruits through highly abbreviated training programs. By 1944, American pilots received two years of training, including at least 300 hours of flight-time, before entering combat, but new Japanese pilots typically received 40 hours of in-flight training or less, and instead of learning navigation, they were simply instructed to tail their group leaders. Looking back, a flight instructor of the time wrote, "Everything was urgent. We were told to rush men through. We abandoned refinements, just tried to teach them how to fly and shoot. One after another, singly, in twos and threes, training planes smashed into the ground, gyrated wildly through the air. For long, tedious months, I tried to create fighter pilots. It was a hopeless task. Our resources were too meagre, the demand too great." (Sakai, 213).

By 1945, the Naval Air Service would run short of volunteers for kamikaze missions, and of the nearly 4,000 kamikaze pilots who perished during the war, a considerable majority were conscripts who enrolled in the program under varying degrees of compulsion. Recruits were trained with torturous regimens or corporal punishment, and stories of mental impairment caused by drugs or saki abound. Some were described as "tottering" and dazed, being carried to their planes by maintenance officers, and forcibly pushed in if they backed down. Pilots who could not find their targets were told to turn around and spare their own lives for another day, but if a pilot returned nine times, he was to be shot. At the moment of collision, he was instructed to keep his eyes open at all times, and to shout "Hissatsu" ("clear kill").

In late 1944, however, the call for volunteers met with considerable enthusiasm among Japanese naval pilots in the Philippines. At a base in Cebu, all but two pilots on staff volunteered for kamikaze missions, and those two holdouts were laid up in the sick bay. One ardent volunteer, Lieutenant Seki Yukio of the 201st Air Group, was a newlywed who had been married for just three months to a woman he had been courting through the mail. "I'm doing this for my beloved wife," he explained to a war correspondent before departing on his final mission. Similarly, before his own final mission on October 28, 1944, Petty Officer Isao Matsuo addressed a letter to his father and mother: "Dear Parents, please congratulate me. I have been given a splendid opportunity to die. This is my last day."

To an outsider, the readiness and outright eagerness of Japanese pilots to accept kamikaze missions may seem profoundly alien, but suicide tactics, though rarely so widespread or organized, were hardly uncommon in warfare. As a 1945 study of the matter by the British Royal

Navy Staff concluded, "Logically, suicide attack in any of the forms, air or sea, practiced by the Japanese, differed only in kind from the last-ditch defense enjoined upon the British after Dunkirk, and only in degree from such missions as the [RAF's 1943] air attack on the Moehne Dam." (Royal Navy, 6:196). What distinguished the *Tokkōtai* program was not necessarily the self-sacrifice it required of its pilots but its scale, its visibility, and its prominent place within the larger Japanese war effort.

Moreover, as the tide of the war turned decisively against Japan, and as casualty counts grew more and more lopsided, the distinction between suicide and conventional missions was not as clear as one might think. Japanese pilots were outnumbered, outgunned, undertrained, and underequipped, so they faced increasingly bleak odds when they flew into combat. For example, the second Japanese air strike of the Battle of the Philippine Sea (June 1944) was comprised of 107 attacking aircraft, and despite being a conventional operation, only 10 survived. With the specter of death already hanging so closely over them, battle-weary Japanese pilots may not have regarded adoption of kamikaze tactics as the profound existential leap it appears to people today.

A kamikaze attempts to hit the USS *White Plains* on October 25

Kamikazes would sink at least 59 Allied vessels and damage over 300 by the end of the war, resulting in minimum casualty figures of 6,805 Americans killed and 9,923 wounded. The actual numbers likely ranged much higher due to lack of precise casualty figures from many ships, particularly those not sunk outright. That said, the rise in the use of kamikaze attacks was evidence of the loss of Japan's air superiority and its waning industrial might. Altogether, nearly 4,000 kamikaze pilots died in combat between October 1944 and August 1945, and about one in seven managed to hit his target. At their peak, they did far more damage to the American Navy than did conventional air attacks, and they undoubtedly placed a significant new obstacle in the path of the American forces slowly encircling the Japanese home islands. Kamikazes were so effective in part because the Zero fighter, reflecting Japanese Imperial values in its total lack of armor protection for the pilot, exploded vigorously on impact and burned furiously thanks to a lack of safety features. Initially, the Navy sought to hide the suicide missions from the American public, explaining the crashes as those of Japanese pilots killed at the controls of their aircraft and then accidentally ramming their targeted vessel. The quaint headlines this produced remain as a testament to an unsuccessful attempt at censorship.

At the same time, the widespread use of kamikaze tactics darkened and hardened attitudes toward Japan within the American military and helped to set the stage for the total war on Japanese civilians that the American military waged in the closing months of the war. *The Marine Corps Gazette* noted, "The ruthless atrocities by the Japanese throughout the war had already brought on an altered behavior (deemed so by traditional standards) by many Americans resulting in the desecration of Japanese remains, but the Japanese tactic of using the Okinawan people as human shields brought about a new aspect of terror and torment to the psychological capacity of the Americans." As one sailor aboard the USS *Miami* recalled about kamikaze attacks at Okinawa, "They came in swarms from all directions. The barrels of our ship's guns got so hot we had to use firehoses to cool them down."

Picture of a kamikaze hitting the USS *Essex* on November 25, 1944

Chapter 8: The End of the War

On February 23, 1945, one of the most famous photographs in American history was taken atop Mount Suribachi, as five American soldiers began to raise an American flag. The picture, which most Americans are instantly familiar with, has come to symbolize the strength and sacrifice of America's armed forces, and though many realize it was taken during the Battle of Iwo Jima, much of the actual battle and the context of the picture itself have been overshadowed.

The Battle of Iwo Jima, code name "Operation Detachment," is more of a misnomer than anything. It was fought as part of a large American invasion directed by steps toward the Japanese mainland, and it was more like a siege that lasted 36 days from February-March 1945, with non-stop fighting every minute. In fact, the iconic flag-raising photo was taken just four days into the battle, and as that picture suggests, the battle was not a pristine tactical event but an unceasing horror with no haven for protection. As veteran and author James F. Christ put it in the foreword of his exhaustive study of the action, "it is carnage…that is what Iwo was…the

Gettysburg of the Pacific." Iwo Jima defined the classical amphibious assault of the World War II era, as much as the Normandy invasion did, but it came later in the war. In Europe, the Battle of the Bulge had already been won, and German forces would surrender in early May. However, the Japanese Empire was still at a considerable level of strength and state of resolve, and an essential offensive, grinding from island to island with naval unit to naval unit and air to air was met with maniacal resistance by the enemy.

Near the end of 1944, as Allied forces were pushing across the Pacific and edging ever closer to Japan, plans were drawn up to invade the Ryuku islands, the most prominent of them being Okinawa. Military planners anticipated that an amphibious campaign would last a week, but instead of facing 60,000 Japanese defenders as estimated, there were closer to 120,000 on the island at the beginning of the campaign in April 1945. The Battle of Okinawa was the largest amphibious operation in the Pacific theater, and it would last nearly 3 months and wind up being the fiercest in the Pacific theater during the war, with nearly 60,000 American casualties and over 100,000 Japanese soldiers killed.

Okinawa witnessed every conceivable horror of war both on land and at sea. American ground forces on Okinawa had to deal with bad weather (including a typhoon), anti-tank moats, barbed wire, mines, caves, underground tunnel networks, and fanatical Japanese soldiers who were willing to use human shields while fighting to the death. Allied naval forces supporting the amphibious invasion had to contend with Japan's notorious kamikazes, suicide pilots who terrorized sailors as they frantically tried to shoot down the Japanese planes before they could hit Allied ships. As one sailor aboard the USS *Miami* recalled, "They came in swarms from all directions. The barrels of our ship's guns got so hot we had to use firehoses to cool them down." As *The Marine Corps Gazette* noted, "More mental health issues arose from the Battle of Okinawa than any other battle in the Pacific during World War II. The constant bombardment from artillery and mortars coupled with the high casualty rates led to a great deal of men coming down with combat fatigue. Additionally the rains caused mud that prevented tanks from moving and tracks from pulling out the dead, forcing Marines (who pride themselves on burying their dead in a proper and honorable manner) to leave their comrades where they lay. This, coupled with thousands of bodies both friend and foe littering the entire island, created a scent you could nearly taste. Morale was dangerously low by the month of May and the state of discipline on a moral basis had a new low barometer for acceptable behavior. The ruthless atrocities by the Japanese throughout the war had already brought on an altered behavior (deemed so by traditional standards) by many Americans resulting in the desecration of Japanese remains, but the Japanese tactic of using the Okinawan people as human shields brought about a new aspect of terror and torment to the psychological capacity of the Americans."

Given the horrific nature of the combat, and the fact that it was incessant for several weeks, it's no surprise that Okinawa had a profound psychological effect on the men who fought, but it also greatly influenced the thinking of military leaders who were planning subsequent campaigns, including a potential invasion of the Japanese mainland. One of the most notable aspects of the battle was the Japanese's determination to fight to the death, but they also forced civilians into fighting and even forced civilians to commit mass suicide when the end was near. A recent documentary has asserted "there were two types of orders for 'honorable deaths' - one for residents to kill each other and the other for the military to kill all residents." As a result, it's believed that over 100,000 civilians may have been killed, a number made all the more difficult to estimate due to the fact that an untold number evacuated into caves and were entombed in them when American soldiers sealed them as they advanced in order to protect themselves. American troops also used flamethrowers to smoke the Japanese out of caves, and in the process, it was impossible to distinguish civilians from soldiers.

Most importantly, the Battle of Okinawa was so ruthless that it convinced Allied leaders that the invasion of Japan would be an absolute bloodbath for all sides. American military officials estimated that there would be upwards of a million Allied casualties if they had to invade the Japanese mainland, and if they were successful, Japan would suffer tens of millions of casualties in the process. As the Battle of Okinawa was about to finish, America's secret Manhattan Project was on the brink of its final goal: a successful detonation of a nuclear device. On July 16, 1945, the first detonation of a nuclear device took place in Alamogordo, New Mexico.

As the defense of Iwo Jima and Okinawa indicated, by 1945, the Japanese government seemed prepared to immolate their own nation rather than surrender. The Americans found many hundreds of suicide mini-submarines, thousands of suicide speedboats, 1,000 suicide diving suits with built-in explosives, and thousands of Oka suicide aircraft – tubes of metal fitted with a 600 mph rocket engine and no landing gear – placed along the coast to meet the invasion force, with more half-completed in the factories. Veterans instructed small children in the use of hand grenades for suicide attacks against American soldiers who would hesitate to shoot at such an individual approaching them.

Reports of these devices and plans, added to civilian mass suicides on Okinawa despite generally civilized treatment by the invading Americans, plus projections of 800,000-1.2 million American casualties within 4 months of landing, prompted President Harry S. Truman to authorize the use of atomic weapons on Hiroshima and Nagasaki. Seeing, perhaps, that their dreams of a final cinematic banzai charge by the entire Japanese people would wither in impersonal blasts of nuclear fire, the Emperor and his generals finally agreed to surrender to the United States.

One of the strangest potential suicide missions planned by the Japanese in the war's closing year involved sending a submarine to the U.S. itself. There, the submarine would ensure delivery of porcelain "flea bombs" containing millions of infectious fleas bred on prisoners in the torture and medical experimentation camps of Japan's horrific Unit 731 biological warfare research department. The Japanese planned for this attack, slated for late September 1945, to be launched "against the American mainland dubbed with the delicate code name 'Cherry Blossoms at Night.' This operation entailed a bubonic plague attack on the city of San Diego, California, in which one of Japan's unique plane-carrying, long-range diesel submarines would stealthily approach America's West Coast and release a small airplane with fold-out wings (the Japanese navy had a minimum of five such subs). The plane would then fly over San Diego and scatter plague-infected fleas." (Barenblatt, 2004, 190-191).

Whether the Japanese would actually carry the plan out remains unknown since the Imperial government decided to surrender in August and finalized the act itself on September 2nd, 1945. The last and potentially most dreadful suicide attack – perhaps leading to massive bombing retribution against the Japanese home islands – failed to materialize as the long struggle finally reached its conclusion.

Chapter 9: The Legacy of Naval Warfare during World War II

World War II represented a final shift away from the age-old preeminence of land warfare and a decisive change in favor of sea power and air power. Nazi Germany produced a magnificently effective land army in the Wehrmacht and the elite Waffen SS units supplementing it, and German armored fighting vehicles outmatched almost all their Allied counterparts except a few late-war designs never present in sufficient numbers to tip the balance. Their superbly trained infantry operated with a tactical finesse that was almost never seen among the Soviets and was superior to that shown by the British and Americans. However, the war proved that strategic and tactical dominance ultimately belonged to the nations focusing their efforts on developing their navies and air forces.

Hitler and his top commanders chose to support the Luftwaffe inadequately and completely eschew the surface fleet and air carrier as major weapons systems. In doing so, they doomed the "Thousand-Year Reich" to a lifespan considerably shorter than a single human generation. American shipping kept the British and Soviets in the war through vast supplies of food and materiel. In conjunction with that, the Anglo-American air forces strangled Germany's tactical and strategic mobility, prevented the movement of critical raw materials, and destroyed many of the vehicles and weapon systems the Nazi factories produced while the Germans were transporting them to the front (between 25% and 50% by 1944).

In the Pacific, the Japanese realized the crucial importance of combined sea and air power. Concentrating their productive capacity on manufacturing aircraft carriers, aircraft, and surface ships rather than tanks, the Empire of Japan developed the IJN into its chief instrument of war. The IJN rivaled the Royal Navy in size, number, and quality of ships, though aircraft technology soon lagged behind the American F6F Hellcat and Mustang. Ultimately, however, the Japanese failed to match the overwhelming industrial capacity of the United States and succumbed to the pressure of the American juggernaut. Japanese anti-aircraft gunners used inaccurate "barrage firing" to the last, while American ships defended themselves with precisely aimed streams of fire that made enemy approaches a lethal proposition even for kamikaze determined to die on the enemy's deck. Radar of increasing sophistication, including radar-guided guns, only added to the Americans' overwhelming power advantage.

The Americans proved the decisive force in World War II, despite the much greater losses sustained in battle by the Soviets and the superior land weaponry of the Germans, due to a calculus involving both geography and emergent technology. Earth's surface consists of 29% land, 71% water, and is 100% covered by air. With their powerful naval and air forces, the United States could potentially project their power more effectively than any other combatant over 71% of the Earth's surface and, after the Luftwaffe's defeat, held the high ground over 100% of it. The Soviets, Japanese, and Germans enjoyed a stronger position over only 29% of the planet at maximum, and the Anglo-American strategic dominance of the sea additionally placed most of the land surface out of their reach.

In essence, much as Yamamoto had feared, the entry of America into the war ultimately ensured Allied victory from the moment the Japanese launched their first torpedo at Pearl Harbor.

Online Resources

Other World War II titles by Charles River Editors

Other titles about the Naval Warfare of World War II on Amazon

Bibliography

Barenblatt, Daniel. *A Plague Upon Humanity: the Hidden History of Japan's Biological Warfare Program.* New York, 2004.

Bornemann, Walter R. *The Admirals: Nimitz, Halsey, Leahy, and King – the Five Star Admirals Who Won the War at Sea.* New York, 2012.

Cox, Jeffrey R. *Rising Sun, Falling Skies: the Disastrous Java Sea Campaign of World War II.* Oxford, 2014.

Forczyk, Robert. *German Commerce Raider vs. British Cruiser.* Long Island City, 2010.

O'Brien, Phillips Payson. *How the War was Won: Air-Sea Power and Allied Victory in World War II.* Cambridge, 2015.

Pitt, Barrie. *The Battle of the Atlantic: World War II.* Morristown, 1977.

Pruitt, Sarah. "WWII's Largest Battleship Revealed After 70 Years Underwater." *History.com,* http://www.history.com/news/wwiis-largest-battleship-revealed-after-70-

<u>years- underwater,</u> March 17, 2015.

Stille, Mark. *USN Carriers vs. IJN Carriers, the Pacific 1942.* Oxford, 2007.

Stille, Mark. *Imperial Japanese Navy Battleships, 1941-45.* Oxford, 2008.

Stille, Mark. *The Coral Sea 1942: the First Carrier Battle.* Oxford, 2009.

Toll, Ian W. *Pacific Crucible: War at Sea in the Pacific, 1941-1942.* New York, 2011.

Vaeth, J. Gordon. *Blimps and U-Boats: U.S. Navy Airships in the Battle of the Atlantic.* Annapolis, 1992.

Wills, Charles A. *Pearl Harbor.* Englewood Cliffs, 1991.

Woodward, C. Vann. *The Battle for Leyte Gulf: the Incredible Story of World War II's Largest Naval Battle.* New York, 2007.

Wooldridge, E.T. *Carrier Warfare in the Pacific: an Oral History Collection.* Washington D.C., 1993.

Zettering, Niklas, and Michael Tamelander. *Bismarck: the Final Days of Germany's Greatest Battleship.* Philadelphia, 2012.

Printed in the USA
CPSIA information can be obtained
at www.ICGtesting.com
LVHW022147260923
759443LV00034B/763